THE NEW DIVISION OF LABOR

THE NEW DIVISION OF LABOR

How Computers Are Creating the Next Job Market

Frank Levy and Richard J. Murnane

RUSSELL SAGE FOUNDATION
New York

PRINCETON UNIVERSITY PRESS
Princeton and Oxford

NEW AGE

First Indian Sub-Continent Edition : 2006
by New Age International (P) Ltd., Publishers

[redacted]

Printed in India at VK Printer, Delhi
1 2 3 4 5 6 7 8 9 10
C-06-04-672

ISBN: 81-224-1884-8
Indian Edition Price: Rs. 195.00
Original Edition Price: $ 39.95

PUBLISHING FOR ONE WORLD

NEW AGE INTERNATIONAL (P) LIMITED, PUBLISHERS
(formerly Wiley Eastern Limited)

New Delhi • Bangalore • Chennai • Cochin • Guwahati • Hyderabad
Jalandhar • Kolkata • Lucknow • Mumbai • Ranchi
Visit us at **www.newagepublishers.com**

CONTENTS

ACKNOWLEDGMENTS

MANY PEOPLE HELPED US DURING THE YEARS THAT WE worked on this book. First and foremost, we thank our friend and colleague David Autor, professor of economics at MIT. David has had a long-standing interest in the impacts of computers on work. In the summer of 1998 the three of us met regularly to develop an understanding of the types of tasks computers can and cannot perform well. Our discussions produced both a good part of the theory that underlies this book and a large joint empirical project in which David led the way. This work resulted in an Autor, Levy, and Murnane article published in the *Quarterly Journal of Economics* in 2003. A nontechnical discussion of much of the evidence in that article is presented in chapter 3 of this book. David also read an early draft of our manuscript and provided comments that were critical to sharpening our arguments.

Thanks go also to Randy Davis and Peter Szolovits, professors at MIT's Computer Science and Artificial Intelligence Laboratory. Starting in early 1998 they answered our beginners' questions with great patience, a patience that eventually allowed us to grasp what they were telling us.

We have an equally large debt to the Alfred P. Sloan Foundation and the Russell Sage Foundation, which provided most of the funding for the research. Hirsh Cohen of Sloan and Eric Wanner, President of Russell Sage, both took a risk that two labor economists, without a long computer track record, could ultimately learn how computers were reshaping work. As our work moved into cognitive psychology, Wanner, with a Ph.D. in cognitive psychology, served as a frequent sounding board, pointing out pieces to read and ideas to explore. We hope both men believe their risk has paid off.

Additional financial support for the project came from MIT's Industrial Performance Center and the MIT-Ford Motor Company Research Collaboration. Levy received other funding from the Daniel Rose Chair in Urban Economics and a one-month fellowship at the Rockefeller Study Center in Bellagio, Italy, and Murnane received support from the Juliana W. and William Foss Thompson Professorship for Education and Society, and from the Spencer Foundation.

The research would not have been possible without people who gave us access to observe in their places of work. They include Gary Abate and Roger Perron, Tom and Rozann Buckner, Andy Cooper, Mary Russo and the teachers at the Murphy School, Jim Soltis and his colleagues at IBM, John Behrens and his colleagues at Cisco Networking Academies, and managers and employees from "Cabot Bank" and "Medford Orbit." Boeing and Fannie Mae also provided useful information.

Other people who helped us by explaining the nature of their work and how computers were affecting it include Tim Guiney, Elliott Mahler, Stephen Saltz, and Jeff Silver. Joan Buchanan provided valuable insight about computers' effects on healthcare.

As our theory was taking shape, we faced the problem of how to tell our story in a way that would be accessible to interested readers. A number of people gave good advice in this regard, including Gene Bardach, Atul Gawande, Chuck Herz, Nick Lemann, Florence Levy, and David Wessell. Special thanks go to Flip Kissam, a professor of law at the University of Kansas, whose broad outlook on life enabled him to dream up the right title for an economists' book.

Still other people read parts or all of draft manuscripts to help correct issues of substance. They include Rosemary Batt, Michael Feuer, Kurt Fischer, Patricia Graham, Ellen Guiney, Neil Heffernan, Jed Kolko, Ellen Lagemann, Richard Lester, Richard and Katherine Nelson, Paul Osterman, Edward Pauly, Thomas Payzant, James Rebitzer, Christine Sanni, and Robert Schwartz.

Several graduate students helped us with research for the book. Thanks go to Anne Beamish, Isabelle Fernandez, Melissa Kearny, Cynthia Perry, Hani Shakeel, and Nancy Sharkey.

Kathleen Donovan, a reference librarian at Harvard's Gutman Library, tracked down numerous references for us, in some cases anticipating what we really wanted to know before we understood it.

We thank Peter Dougherty, the social science editor at Princeton University Press, his colleague Tim Sullivan, and Suzanne Nichols of the Russell Sage Foundation for pushing us to clarify the book's message and shepherding the manuscript to publication.

Richard Murnane's secretary, Wendy Angus, patiently kept track of the multiple versions of chapters and made sure that the right versions were sent to readers and to Peter.

We dedicate this book to our families. Our children, David, Marin, John, and Daniel, would tease us about this book's movie rights, but their good humor (most of the time) kept us going. Florence Levy gave us good skeptical questions and a mother's encouragement. Most of all, we thank our wives, Katherine Swartz and Mary Jo Murnane, for sharing their lives with us and for always being there for us.

THE NEW DIVISION OF LABOR

CHAPTER 1

New Divisions of Labor

ON MARCH 22, 1964, THE AD HOC COMMITTEE ON THE TRIPLE Revolution sent a fourteen-page memorandum to President Lyndon Johnson. The signers included chemist Linus Pauling (recipient of two Nobel Prizes), economist Gunnar Myrdal (a future Nobel Prize-winner), and Gerard Piel, publisher of *Scientific American*. In the memo, the committee warned the president of long-run threats to the nation beginning with the likelihood that computers would soon create mass unemployment.

> A new era of production has begun. Its principles of organization are as different from those of the industrial era as those of the industrial era were different from the agricultural. The cybernation revolution has been brought about by the combination of the computer and the automated self-regulating machine. This results in a system of almost unlimited productive capacity which requires progressively less human labor. Cybernation is already reorganizing the economic and social system to meet its own needs.[1]

In one respect the committee's warning was prophetic. Computers now replace humans in carrying out an ever widening range of tasks—

filing, bookkeeping, mortgage underwriting, taking book orders, installing windshields on automobile bodies—the list becomes longer each year. And beyond directly replacing humans, computers have become the infrastructure of the global economy, helping jobs move quickly to sources of cheap labor.

But the Ad Hoc Committee also made a major miscalculation. Like many computer scientists of that time, the committee expected computers would soon replicate all the modes by which humans process information. The expectation was only partly fulfilled, and so the committee's warning was only partly right. Computers have not created mass unemployment, but they have created a major upheaval in the nature of human work.

More than two centuries ago, Adam Smith used the words "division of labor" to describe an earlier upheaval—the way in which the first factory systems had reorganized work and dramatically boosted productivity.[2] In today's economy, Smith's words have taken on new meanings. There is a new division of labor between people and computers. And there is a growing division within human labor itself—a divide between those who can and those who cannot do valued work in an economy filled with computers. Bridging this divide involves more than ensuring that the affluent and the poor have access to the same hardware and software. It involves rethinking education and training, beginning with answering four fundamental questions:

- What kinds of tasks do humans perform better than computers?
- What kinds of tasks do computers perform better than humans?
- In an increasingly computerized world, what well-paid work is left for people to do both now and in the future?
- How can people learn the skills to do this work?

Answering these questions is the focus of this book.

HOW WORK HAS CHANGED

One day in June 2003, a General Electric technician made a service call to a suburban house to check on a malfunctioning ice-maker. As he was writing up the receipt for the repair, he apologized for having had to call for directions thirty minutes before he arrived.

> I carry maps but the work order didn't even have your street address. It just had "HOUSE" and your phone number. The problem is that they've just switched our call center from India to Costa Rica. They're still learning the procedures down there and they must be having trouble with addresses.

The explanation was plausible—a call center that used operators who read scripts on computer screens moved to a source of even cheaper labor. In fact, however, the work order had not been taken by a human operator but by a computer using speech recognition software. By reading menus to the caller, the software could prompt the caller to identify the problem as being in a refrigerator, specifically, the ice-maker. It could also prompt the caller to choose a time he would be at home from a list of times when technicians were available. The speech recognition software could recognize the caller's phone number and establish that the home address was a "HOUSE" rather than an apartment. While the software was not yet good enough to recognize the home address itself, it had captured enough information to print up a work order and append it to the technician's schedule.

In 1990 that work order would have been taken by an operator sitting somewhere in the United States. That operator's job is now gone. Whether the job was displaced by a computer or a Costa Rican call center is unimportant for the moment. What is important is that the loss of the operator's job is part of a much larger pattern.

As recently as 1970, more than one-half of employed U.S. adults worked in two broad occupational categories: blue-collar jobs and clerical jobs (including the operator who would have written up the work order). Few people got rich in these jobs, but they supported middle- and lower-middle-class living and many were open to high school graduates. Today, less than 40 percent of adults have blue-collar or clerical jobs and many of these jobs require at least some college education. The computerization of work has played a significant role in this change.

Had the rest of the economy remained unchanged, the declining importance of blue-collar and clerical jobs might have resulted in the rising unemployment feared by the Ad Hoc Committee. But computers are Janus-faced, helping to create jobs even as they destroy jobs. As computers have helped channel economic growth, two quite different types of jobs have increased in number, jobs that pay very different wages. Jobs held by the working poor—janitors, cafeteria workers, security guards—have grown in relative importance.[3] But the greater job growth has taken place in the upper part of the pay distribution—managers, doctors, lawyers, engineers, teachers, technicians. Three facts about these latter jobs stand out: they pay well, they require extensive skills, and most people in these jobs rely on computers to increase their productivity. This hollowing-out of the occupational structure—more janitors and more managers—is heavily influenced by the computerization of work.

Beneath the level of the job title, computers are rearranging tasks *within* jobs. The secretary's job provides a prime example. Even as there are relatively fewer secretaries, the job itself is changing. A quarter century ago, the U.S. Department of Labor *Occupational Outlook* described a secretary's job in this way:

> Secretaries relieve their employers of routine duties so they can work on more important matters. Although most secretaries type, take shorthand, and deal with callers, the time spent on these duties varies in different types of organizations.

Compare the description of the same job in today's *Occupational Outlook:*

> As technology continues to expand in offices across the Nation, the role of the secretary has greatly evolved. Office automation and organizational restructuring have led secretaries to assume a wide range of new responsibilities once reserved for managerial and professional staff. Many secretaries now provide training and orientation to new staff, conduct research on the Internet, and learn to operate new office technologies. In the midst of these changes, however, their core responsibilities have remained much the same—performing and coordinating an office's administrative activities and ensuring that information is disseminated to staff and clients.

What is true for secretaries is true for many other jobs. In the chapters ahead we will explain why computerized work has increased the value of identifying and solving uncharted problems—work that we call "expert thinking." We will also explain why computerized work has increased the importance of "complex communication," conveying not just information but *a particular interpretation of information*.

At the same time, we will see that the ability to apply well-understood routines to solve problems is not valued as it used to be. Twenty years ago, a man or woman could make a good living as a mortgage underwriter, accepting and rejecting loan applications. That work is now almost entirely computerized.

DIFFERENT KINDS OF THINKING

A first step toward understanding these patterns begins with the Ad Hoc Committee's mistake. Start with the fact that all human work involves the cognitive processing of information. The analyst who reads revenue numbers in a spreadsheet, the farmer who looks to the sky for signs of rain, the chef who tastes a sauce, the carpenter who feels his hammer as it hits a nail—all these men and women are processing information to decide what to do next or to update their picture of the world.

For most of economic history, technical innovation involved machines replacing humans in performing *physical* tasks—the shift of weaving from artisans' hands to mechanical looms, the shift of long-distance messaging from Pony Express riders to the telegraph. Through all of these changes, *cognitive* tasks—the information processing that is a part of all work—remained a largely human province.[4] With the 1945 advent of the ENIAC, the first programmable computer, *some* information processing could now be done by "machines that can think."

The Ad Hoc Committee predicted a jobless economy because it had ignored the word *some*. We take for granted that a truck—not a person—is best to carry a set of living room furniture from a showroom to a house. But a person—not a machine—is best to change a newborn's diaper. In a similar way, computers have the advantage over humans in carrying out tasks that involve *some* kinds of information processing. But humans retain an advantage over computers in tasks requiring other kinds of information processing. At any moment in time, the boundary marking human advantage over computers largely defines the area of useful human work.[5]

This boundary shifts as computer scientists expand what computers can do, but as we will see, it continues to move in the same direction, increasing the importance of expert thinking and complex communication as the domains of well-paid human work. What is true about today's rising skill requirements will be even more true tomorrow.

Who will have the skills to do the good jobs in an economy filled with computers? Those who do not will be at the bottom of an increasingly unequal income distribution—the working poor. The disappearance of clerical and blue-collar jobs from the lower middle of the pay distribution illustrates this pattern of limited job options. People with sufficient workplace skills can move from these jobs into one of the expanding sets of higher-wage jobs. People who lack the right skills drop down to compete for unskilled work at declining wages.

This dynamic, repeated in many workplaces, has contributed to the extraordinary growth over the past twenty-five years in the earnings gap between college graduates and high school graduates. In 1979, the average thirty-year-old man with a bachelor's degree earned just 17 percent more than a thirty-year-old man with a high school diploma. Today, the equivalent college-high school wage gap exceeds 50 percent, and the gap for women is larger. Employers judge that college graduates are more likely than high school graduates to have the skills needed to do the jobs requiring expert thinking and complex communication.

The national challenge is to recognize the inexorable changes in the job distribution and to prepare young people with the skills needed in the growing number of good jobs. As we explain in the chapters that follow, these skills include the ability to bring facts and relationships to bear in problem solving, the ability to judge when one problem-solving strategy is not working and another should be tried, and the ability to engage in complex communication with others.

GRASPING THE RIGHT PROBLEM

The story we tell differs from most other popular accounts of how computers affect human work. Accounts that focused on *individual users* were often utopian, describing the unlimited gains computers could bring to the workplace. But accounts that focused on the *entire economy* frequently carried the Ad Hoc Committee's warning of mass unemployment. It is easy to see why. When the Ad Hoc Committee wrote its memo, a computer could already play a good game of chess—a sophisticated task for a person. It was easy to assume that computers would soon master simple tasks like making one's way across a crowded room to select an apple from a bowl of fruit, something four-year-olds could do. The logical next step would be to subsume all human work.

As we will see, the trip for the apple has proved extremely difficult to program—the problem is yet to be solved. But neither this difficulty nor the continued growth of jobs has put the unemployment fear to rest. In 1995, science writer Jeremy Rifkin argued that computer-driven unemployment was already upon us:

> In the past, when new technologies have replaced workers in a given sector, new sectors have always emerged to absorb the displaced laborers. Today, all three of the traditional sectors of the economy—agriculture, manufacturing, and service—are experiencing technological displacement, forcing millions onto the unemployment rolls. The only new sector emerging is the knowledge sector, made up of elite entrepreneurs, scientists, technicians, computer programmers, professionals, educators, and consultants. While this sector is growing, it is not expected to absorb more than a fraction of the hundreds of millions who will be eliminated in the next several decades in the wake of revolutionary advances in the information and communication sciences.[6]

As Rifkin was writing, other analysts were making more refined predictions of job loss. Michael Hammer, a founder of the re-engineering movement, argued that computer-driven re-engineering would "obliterate" large numbers of management jobs. Neil Rackham, a prolific author on salesmanship, predicted that web-based e-commerce would radically reduce the number of sales jobs.[7] None of these predictions has come to pass.

Hindsight makes everything obvious, but better predictions existed even as the Ad Hoc Committee was writing. A decade earlier, Peter Drucker had published *The Practice of Management,* the book that established his reputation as a preeminent management theorist. Drucker predicted computers would affect jobs, but not through mass unemployment:

> The technological changes now occurring will carry [the Industrial Revolution] a big step further. They will not make human labor superfluous. On the contrary, they will require tremendous numbers of highly skilled and highly trained men—managers to think through and plan, highly trained technicians and workers to design the new tools, to produce them, to maintain them, to direct them. Indeed, the major obstacle to the rapid spread of these changes will almost certainly be the lack, in every country, of enough trained men.[8]

Many writers could have profited from reading Drucker. But had someone offered a prize for foretelling the future, Herbert Simon would have won it for his obscure 1960 essay, "The Corporation: Will It Be Managed by Machines?"

Herbert Simon himself was far from obscure. Over his career, he established international reputations in economics (winning a Nobel Prize), organizational behavior, artificial intelligence, and psychology. With this background, he was perfectly positioned to understand the interplay between computers and work. But his 1960 essay was issued under modest circumstances, a chapter in a symposium volume marking the tenth anniversary of his institution, the Graduate School of Industrial Administration of the Carnegie Institute of Technology (now Carnegie-Mellon University). It was not among the best known of his many writings.

In the essay, Simon explained why computerized work would lead not to mass unemployment but rather to substantial shifts in the economy's mix of jobs. He explained why these shifts would involve movement away from blue-collar and clerical work (something we have already seen). And finally, he offered this prediction:

> [I]n the entire occupied population, a larger fraction of members than at present will be engaged in occupations where "personal service" involving face-to-face human interaction is an important part of the job. I am confident of stating this conclusion; far less confident in conjecturing what these occupations will be.[9]

Unlike many other technology prophets, Simon was largely right. We return to his predictions in the chapters that follow.

THE PLAN OF THE BOOK

We have argued that computers' real impact on work is hollowing out the occupational distribution. The result is a significant increase in the demand for people who perform jobs requiring expert thinking and complex communication. Both U.S. firms and the nation as a whole ignore at their peril how computers are raising the cognitive bar.

In the chapters that follow, we make our case in three parts. In Part I—Computers and the Economy—we explain the kinds of information-processing tasks in which computers dominate humans and the tasks for which the opposite is true (chapter 2). We then show how both the economy's occupational structure and the work done within occupations have changed over the past thirty-five years and the critical role computerization has played in bringing about these changes (chapter 3).

In Part II—The Skills Employers Value—we use workplace examples to describe the two kinds of tasks that computers make more valuable and the skills humans need in order to be good at these tasks. We first examine expert thinking—solving new problems for which there are no routine solutions (chapter 4). We next examine complex communication—persuading, explaining, and in other ways conveying a particular interpretation of information (chapter 5).

In Part III—How Skills Are Taught—we examine how people can learn to become proficient at expert thinking and complex communication. We begin by explaining why strong literacy and numeracy are preconditions (chapter 6). We next describe how corporations are teaching the skills critical to complex communication and expert thinking (chapter 7). We then turn to elementary school classrooms to show what is needed if the standards-based educational reforms now sweeping the country are to prepare American students to thrive in computerized workplaces (chapter 8). Along the way, we show why an emphasis on education for earning a good living does not necessarily conflict with the education needed to be a contributing citizen in a democracy where computers raise issues of privacy, workplace monitoring, and the length of the workday.

In chapter 9, we conclude by addressing whether our story and prescriptions have staying power. We explain why the evolutionary path of work we have described in this book is likely to persist for some time. The result is a polarized job market. Good jobs will increasingly require expert thinking and complex communication. Jobs that do not require these tasks will not pay a living wage. Preparing the work force to deal with this reality presents a formidable economic problem. Broadly shared prosperity—the American dream—depends on the problem's solution.

1

COMPUTERS AND THE ECONOMY

CHAPTER 2

Why People Still Matter

A STORY OF TWO JOBS

On Friday, November 11, 1999, the London International Financial Futures and Options Exchange (Liffe) closed its trading pits. Three days later Liffe reopened for business but its trading pits were empty. Bond dealers now traded directly from their offices using Eurex, a digital trading network based in Frankfurt's Deutsche Bourse. Between Friday and Monday, a hundred open-outcry traders in the pits had lost their jobs.

The traders had cut a vivid picture in their striped jackets, yelling and waving bond dealers' order slips. They also had been well paid. Doug Fisher, a thirty-nine-year-old Liffe trader, had earned the equivalent of $450,000 in his best year.[1] That was in the mid-1990s when 1,000 traders were working in the Liffe pits. But in 1998, Eurex outbid Liffe for what had been Liffe's most important market: the futures contract for the German government's ten-year bond. Eurex's lower trading costs put Liffe under constant pressure. Trading in bond futures boomed, but dealers increasingly traded over Eurex, bypassing the pits. A Liffe trader's commission fell from 1 pound 20 pence per contract to 10 pence.[2] Many traders left the business. Doug Fisher, who stayed, saw his income fall by two-thirds. The closure of Liffe's trading pits became a foregone conclusion. The computerized network had taken the pit traders' jobs.

The demise of the Liffe Traders illustrates one result of computerized work. We can see another result in the office of Dr. Stephen Saltz, a Boston cardiologist. In September 2001, Dr. Saltz took an echocardiogram of an elderly male patient we will call Harold. Harold had suffered a small heart attack. His condition was complicated by diabetes, a disease that creates "silent" heart blockages not detected in standard tests.

When Saltz had trained in Boston's Brigham Hospital in the early 1970s, an echocardiograph was an oscilloscope-like device that provided limited information on the heart's blood flow and valve flaps. Over time, advances in computerization allowed the instrument to create a full two-dimensional image of virtually all aspects of the heart's functioning, including blood flows, blockages, and valve leakages. Using this image, Saltz saw that the entire front wall of Harold's heart was malfunctioning. The information led Saltz to refer Harold to a surgeon who would perform a bypass or insert a stent. Either operation would improve the length and quality of Harold's life. The computerized imaging had made Saltz a better diagnostician.

In the language of economics, computers *substituted* for the Liffe traders' market-making and *complemented* Saltz's diagnostic skills. Why this pair of outcomes? How could computers outperform human bond traders while a human doctor was still required to read an echocardiogram?

RULES

The answer to these questions begins in the ways humans process different kinds of information. In cognitive terms, information is any stimulus that helps us to make sense of the world. The Liffe traders processed price and quantity information to make their buy-and-sell decisions. To make his diagnosis, Saltz processed information contained in Harold's words, appearance, and echocardiogram results. A quarterly earnings estimate, the expression on a customer's face, the tone of a boss' voice—we perceive and process all of this information in the course of daily work. In a general sense, we have been information workers since the dawn of civilization.

Because information and work are inseparable, any technology that changes how we use information has the potential to reorganize how work is done. Early information technologies—talking drums, the telegraph, and telephone—increased the speed at which information could be transmitted, and, in some cases, the gains were remarkable. Just before the advent of the telegraph, sending a one-page message from New York to Chicago took ten days. By 1850, the telegraph had reduced that time to five minutes and had reduced the cost by a factor of 100. The gain in transmission speed supported numerous innovations: creation of the first national stock markets, a revolution in railroad track layouts, the first just-in-time inventory systems.[3]

The computer's advance over earlier technologies is its ability to actually process certain kinds of information. In some cases information processing results in instructions that are sufficient to perform workplace tasks—for instance, guiding an assembly-line robot inserting windshields on pick-up trucks. In other cases, the computer processes one form of information into another, more useful form—for example, a spreadsheet model that processes construction costs and rents into the rate of return on a projected office building, or the software that processes a stream of digital information into a picture of your grandchild. While humans could do all these processing tasks—even creating the grandchild's picture—computers can do them more rapidly and at lower cost.[4]

This way of thinking about computers—as a potential substitute for human information processing—gets us a step closer to the answer we are seeking. Think of any task in the workplace: deciding to buy a bond future contract at a particular price, interpreting an echocardiogram, adding a column of numbers, installing the windshield on the frame of a pick-up truck, painting a picture of the Grand Teton Mountains, mediating a customer complaint, vacuuming a floor in a room crowded with furniture. Each task involves some kind of information processing. But which kinds of information processing can computers do better than people? Answering this question is the key to understanding why Saltz has a thriving cardiology practice while Liffe traders aren't trading any more.

A first answer is that computers' comparative advantage over people lies in tasks that can be described using rules-based logic: step-by-step procedures with an action specified for every contingency. "Rules-based logic" is not an everyday expression, but humans use rules to process information every day. Most of us learned arithmetic using such rules ("If the numbers in the 1's column add to ten or more, carry the . . ."). Recipes in *The Joy of Cooking* are largely based on rules. Most appliance manuals contain instructions using such rules ("If the VCR is not recording, then press "Stop" and press "Record" again. If the VCR still does not record, call 1-800 . . .).

Rules-based logic is equally common in workplace tasks. Consider the case of the mortgage underwriter who decides whether a mortgage application should be approved. At one time, underwriters processed applications using explicit rules in sequence. In the sequence, a rule governing the maximum loan size might be written as

$$\text{If } \frac{\text{[Requested Loan Amount]}}{\text{[Assessed Value of House]}} > 80\%, \text{ Reject the Application.}$$

That is, if the size of the requested loan exceeds 80 percent of the house's assessed value, the underwriter should reject the application. If the application passed this test, the underwriter would then apply the next rule on the list, perhaps an income test that looked like this:

$$\text{If } \frac{\text{[Monthly Mortgage Payment]}}{\text{[Monthly Income]}} > 30\%, \text{ Reject the Application.}$$

The full list of rules might include tests on the applicant's liquid assets, the number of years with the current employer, and so on. An application that passed every test was approved.

Each rule leads to a clean "yes / no" answer and by setting "yes" = 1 and "no" = 0, it is easy to imagine how a computer could be programmed to process mortgage applications in this way. The downside of this sequence of rules is its inflexibility. By applying the rules one by one, a request for a mortgage equal to 85 percent of the house value would be rejected even if the monthly mortgage payment were only 15 percent of the applicant's income.[5] For this reason, underwriters began to adopt a more flexible processing method in which they combined application information into an overall picture that they then would accept or reject.

At first glance, this balancing process would seem hard to capture in rules. However, this is not true. Fannie Mae's Desktop Underwriter®, a program widely used by mortgage brokers, is one among a number of underwriting programs that balances factors in exactly this way.[6] Before writing the program, Fannie Mae statisticians analyzed a large sample of previously approved mortgages. Using statistical techniques, they estimated the relative importance of numerous application items in predicting whether a mortgage had defaulted in its first four years.[7] The result is a mortgage scoring model, a formula that awards points based on the most predictive items including the size of the mortgage; the value of the house; the applicant's income, debts, liquid assets and any prior bankruptcies; the length of the requested mortgage; and so on. The procedure is flexible because low points for some items can be offset by high points on other items in calculating a total point score. Once calculated, an application's total score is compared to at least two threshold values in a block of rules that has the general form indicated in box 2.1.

In this software code, the number before each statement is an address, and the "If" statements represent rules-based tests. If the application

BOX 2.1

Decision Stage of a Mortgage Scoring Model

```
10 If (Mortgage Score > Threshold 1), Go to 20
11 If (Mortgage Score > Threshold 2), Go to 22
12 Application Status = Reject
13 Go to 25
20 Application Status = Approved
21 Go to 25
22 Application Status = Refer with Caution
25 Print Application Result
```

passes the test, the program jumps to the specified address. If the application fails the test, the program drops down to the next statement. Statement 10 states that if the application's score exceeds Threshold 1 (the higher of the two thresholds), the program goes to Statement 20, where Application Status is rated "Approved," and then the result is printed. If the application's score does not exceed Threshold 1, the program drops down to Statement 11, where the score is compared to the lower Threshold 2. If the score exceeds Threshold 2—that is, the score lies between Threshold 1 and Threshold 2—the Application Status is set to "Refer with Caution," a rating meaning the application is on the borderline between approval and denial and requires human judgment. (Other parts of the program, not shown here, can also trigger requests for human judgment.) If the application score is less than Threshold 2, the application is rated "Reject" and the result is printed.

If we step back from the detail, we see the program (like the human underwriter) is *processing* information—converting information on the application form into a recommendation to accept or reject the application. If computers executed rules slowly, mortgage applications would still be processed by people. In fact, computers execute rules much faster than humans and so mortgage underwriting is largely a computerized job.

In the case of mortgage underwriting, processing leads directly to a decision. We said earlier that we can also process information to update our picture of the world with no immediate action. An underwriting-like example would be a set of rules that converted a person's financial information into an updated credit rating.

We now know enough to start answering our questions. The Eurex trading network could substitute for the Liffe traders because trading in the pits could be expressed as a rules-based task. The trading pits were constructed to bring many dealers' orders together to create a liquid market. Traders with orders to buy or sell within a certain price range looked for an appropriate match, a process that could be specified in rules. Once the Eurex network connected multiple dealers directly, dealers could submit bids electronically into a virtual liquid market where buy and sell orders were matched by software, without bearing the expense of traders and pits.[8]

We can also see that rules-based logic must have limits since rules-based software could not substitute for Stephen Saltz's diagnostic skills. It is to those limits that we now turn.

WHAT RULES CAN'T DO

In a short time we could write a long list of the tasks performed by rules-based software: mortgage underwriting, inventory control, word processing, presentation graphics, flying 777's, on-line book purchasing, and on and on. Some of these tasks involve work that people used to do. Other tasks involve new work that people could not do until computers made it technically feasible—putting music on compact disks. Still other new work had been technically feasible—decoding the genome by hand, for example—but it took computers to make it financially feasible.

Despite its power, rules-based logic suffers from two limits, one important, the other profound. First is the inability to deal with new problems—problems unanticipated by the writer of the rules. Recall the requirement that rules-based logic specify an action for every contingency. If an unforeseen contingency arises, the rules will likely reach a dead end. The problem occurs with some frequency in automobile repair shops. A customer brings in a newly purchased minivan with a nonfunctioning power seat. A technician uses a computerized tool to diagnose the problem. The software in the tool conducts If-Then-Do tests to search for problems that engineers have foreseen: a faulty switch, a break in the wire connecting the switch to the seat motor, a faulty seat motor, and so on. But in a new car, the many electronic components can interact in ways engineers did not foresee. If the seat problem is caused by one of these interactions, the factory-programmed rules will detect no error and the technician will be on his own.

The second, more profound limit is summarized in Michael Polanyi's felicitous phrase, "We can know more than we can tell."[9] Polanyi is referring to what psychologists call intuitive or tacit knowledge—knowledge that we use but cannot articulate.

To grasp Polanyi's idea, we can contrast what in essence are two extremes: a student adding a column of numbers and a bakery truck driver making a left turn against traffic.

The student doing addition is processing a set of numbers by consciously applying rules: 7 + 3 = 10. The rules are what allow the addition to be programmed. The bakery truck driver is processing a constant stream of information from his environment: visual information on traffic light signals, visual and aural information on the trajectories of children, dogs, and other cars, aural information on unseen vehicles (perhaps including sirens), tactile information on the performance of the truck's engine, transmission, and brakes. To program this behavior, we could begin with a video camera and other sensors to capture the sensory input. But executing a left turn across oncoming traffic involves so many factors that it is hard to imagine discovering the set of rules that can replicate the driver's behavior. There are, of course, many cases between these extremes, a point we shall return to shortly.

In the early days of computer science, the obstacle of tacit knowledge was not so apparent. By the mid-1960s, a computer using rules-based logic could play competent chess—a difficult task for humans. Based on this success, many researchers thought software replicating human visual recognition and motor control would come easily. Recall the example from chapter 1—a four-year-old child walking across a crowded room to pick an apple from a bowl of fruit. It was easy to imagine a robot soon doing the same thing.

It turned out otherwise, and we now can start to see why. The four-year-old's walk, like the truck driver's left turn, poses major challenges. We don't know in advance where the girl will find obstacles or what they will look like. We don't know what kind of bowl we are looking for or where the apple will be in the bowl. In the absence of predictability, the number of contingencies explodes as does the knowledge required to deal with them. The required rules are very hard to write. Giving an inspiring speech, designing a new chair, administering anesthesia to a patient—these and many other tasks rely on tacit knowledge and pose limits on computer substitution.

There are some strategies for pushing back on these limits. In chapter 1, we cited Herbert Simon's prescient 1960 essay on how computers would affect occupations. In the essay, Simon observed that it is possible to extend the range of computer substitution by simplifying the task. On an automotive assembly line, a computerized robot arm installs a windshield on the body of a pick-up truck. At first glance, installing a windshield raises the same problems as the four-year-old's walk for the apple. But engineers have simplified the assembly line problem by ensuring that at the point of installation, each truck body and windshield pallet occupy precise positions. This regularity drastically reduces the possible range of movement and allows a computer to perform a task formerly handled by humans.

A different way to expand computer substitution is to consider not the whole job but those tasks within a job that can be expressed in rules. We cannot write If-Then-Do rules that describe how a bank teller puts a nervous customer at ease. But we can write the rules for three of a teller's tasks—accepting deposits, paying out withdrawals, and checking balances—and the software using these rules powers ATM machines. As a result, computers substitute for tellers in much of this routine money handling, while tellers spend more time providing other services.

A third way to expand substitution *for American workers* is to use computers to support outsourcing jobs to other countries. Examples are numerous. Computerized bar codes and order tracking reduce the risk of dealing with overseas suppliers. Computerized scripts and databases allow call centers to be moved abroad. But computer substitution and outsourcing also converge at a deeper level.

Recall the work orders for GE repair technicians (chapter 1). At different times, these work orders were prepared by human operators in India and by a computer. This overlap is no accident. The operator's job involved collecting a restricted set of information—the type of appliance, the general problem, when the customer would be home, and so on. Because the information was restricted, the job could be scripted and performed by an operator who knew little about the United States. But the limited nature of the required information also meant that the job could largely be expressed in software and so performed by a computer.[10] In chapter 3, we shall see how a similar convergence between computers and outsourcing occurs in manufacturing. Taken together, these examples make an important point: *computer substitution and outsourcing are affecting many of the same occupations.*

Despite these various extensions, in a great many jobs human information processing cannot be expressed in rules. It is to these jobs that we turn next.

PATTERNS

What we know now is that Stephen Saltz, the bakery truck driver, and the four-year-old girl all processed information using something other than rules-based logic. This raises two new questions. When humans *don't* appear to use rules to process information, what processing method are they using? And why can't this alternative processing method be programmed on computers?

The answers involve pattern recognition. An example clarifies the idea. In the mid-1980s, the mathematician Stuart Dreyfus conducted an experiment in which Julio Kaplan, an international chess master, played speed chess—with five seconds per move—against a slightly weaker opponent.[11] At the same time, a third person standing in the room read random digits aloud at the rate of one digit per second. Kaplan was asked to win the game while keeping a running total of the digits in his head. He did both.

Every novice knows that chess can be played according to a set of rules—"Don't exchange a bishop for a knight"—and versions of these rules are often the basis for chess-playing software. But Kaplan had no time to apply rules: hearing each digit and adding it to the total took most of his conscious thought in each five-second interval. Dreyfus' experiment (and others we discuss in chapter 4) suggests that Kaplan processed the board's information by instantaneously recognizing the pattern of the pieces. Recognition triggered the next move.[12]

The Dreyfus experiment helps to answer the first of our new questions. When Stephen Saltz interpreted the echocardiogram, he was searching for patterns—matching the image on the screen against echocardiogram images stored in his memory. His recognition of a particular pattern helped him to form a diagnosis. Pattern recognition is an equally plausible description of how the truck driver and the four-year-old girl processed what they saw and heard. But notice that in most of these cases, people are recognizing something closer to a concept—what psychologists call a schema—than a precise template. We expect the four-year-old girl to recognize a blue oval bowl even if she so far has seen only green and red round bowls. Stephen Saltz and the truck driver have the same ability to generalize.

Within cognitive science, pattern recognition is a more controversial processing model than rules-based logic. Some researchers argue that if we could peer deeply enough into people's minds, we would find that what we call pattern recognition rests on a series of deeply embedded rules—not the If-Then-Do rules of rules-based logic but probability rules that use information to guess at a likely concept—"that blue oval glass thing filled with fruit is probably a bowl," or, "that high wailing sound is probably a fire engine's siren." Because of this possibility, cognitive scientists disagree about whether pattern recognition is a truly distinct processing method or a processing method that relies on rules that we cannot articulate.[13] But just as rules-based logic offers a useful description of the mortgage underwriter's processing, pattern recognition offers a useful description of Saltz's processing of the echocardiogram—as well as much of the information processing that we all do.

Pattern recognition is also important in the process of creating something new through what cognitive psychologists call "case-based reasoning." For example, an advertising writer is asked to develop a campaign for a new spaghetti sauce. She has never done an ad campaign for spaghetti sauce, but she has done ad campaigns for other quick-to-prepare meals and her knowledge of those cases gives her a useful starting point for thinking about the sauce.[14]

We do much of our creative work in this style: we use pattern recognition to see similarities between a new problem and relevant past work, call that past work to mind, and appropriately apply the knowledge gained in doing that work. In this case, pattern recognition occurs in seeing the points of similarity between the current problem and past experience.

If the focus of this book were cognitive psychology, we would include still other models of human information processing. But for our focus—how computers alter work—a short list of models including rules-based-logic, pattern recognition, and case-based reasoning (pattern recognition's first cousin) serves quite well.

THE LIMITS OF PATTERN RECOGNITION

If we take a step back, we can see that we are well along in answering the questions we have raised:

- Computers excel at processing information through the application of rules.
- Computers could substitute for the Liffe traders because the information processing required to match buy and sell orders (the main task of the floor traders) could be fully described in step-by-step rules.
- Stephen Saltz processed the information in the echocardiogram by recognizing patterns rather than applying step-by-step rules.

One question remains: if pattern recognition is so central to human work, why can't we program computers to do it? In fact, we can program computers to recognize patterns—but two problems limit this recognition to restricted contexts.

First is the problem of perception. The four-year-old begins her walk with a two-dimensional set of photons projected onto her retina. To make sense of what she sees, she must extract features from this information, understanding where an adult's legs end and where another object begins. In a complex visual field, this feature extraction is extremely difficult to program even though most four-year-olds do it without thinking. Perception is an equally difficult problem in speech recognition, determining where words begin and end, factoring out the "ummm's" and "like's."

The second problem, for both people and computers, involves interpreting what is perceived—recognizing what it is we are seeing, hearing, tasting, and so on. This recognition involves comparing what is perceived to concepts or schemas stored in memory. The schemas in Stephen Saltz's memory are the product of extensive study and experience. Had Harold's echocardiogram been shown to a second-year medical student, the student might have arrived at a diagnosis, but the diagnosis might well have been wrong.

Problems arise because schemas can require vast quantities of knowledge, including knowledge we overlook because we take it for granted. In the mid-1960s one of this book's authors took his two-year old goddaughter and her parents to the observation deck of Boston's then-new Prudential Center. As the adults marveled at the street views below, the goddaughter banged her hands on the glass trying to reach the toy cars she saw just beyond the window.[15] On the basis of visual information alone, the goddaughter and the adults each had a point. The image could have been real cars and people 700 feet below or toy cars and 1/4-inch tall people just beyond the window.

Standing on the observation deck, the adults resolved this ambiguity by applying previously acquired knowledge. They ruled out toy cars (without consciously thinking about it) because they knew from experience that a four-minute ride on an express elevator leaves you high above the street and people and cars look small at that distance. They also knew from experience that 1/4-inch-tall people did not exist. The two-year-old goddaughter knew no such things.

These schemas—stored facts and relationships—act as a context in which we process all new information, not just visual images. Suppose in the course of conversation, a friend says the word "BILL." How do we interpret it? As a person's first name? As the front end of a duck? As a piece of legislation? As a request for payment? As a piece of currency? The answer will depend on the context of the conversation. If the person is speaking about her male cousin, we will probably interpret "BILL" as a person's first name unless she is speaking about her cousin's financial problems, in which case we may have to listen more closely.

When we try to program pattern recognition, problems of perception and the requirements for contextual knowledge limit what we can recognize. In technical terms, pattern recognition is programmed using neural nets and other "machine learning" software. These methods are based on the conjecture advanced earlier that human pattern recognition itself may rest on probabilistic rules. Recall that in programs using rules-based logic, the explicit rules can be stated before the program is ever written. In the case of Fannie Mae's Desktop Underwriter, the analysis of previously issued mortgages provided the points assessed to different pieces of information in computing a total score. By contrast, in neural net software, the program is "trained" on samples of previously identified patterns to "learn" which characteristics of a set of information mark it as a pattern of interest. For example, training would enable speech recognition software to distinguish the digital pattern of the spoken word "BILL" from the digital pattern of "ROSE" and to distinguish each of them from the digital pattern for "SPAGHETTI." But once software has identified "BILL," there is still the problem of determining which meaning of "BILL" is intended.

An everyday example is the *Graffiti*® handwriting recognition software in the Palm OS®. Like the assembly-line robot, the software's task is simplified by requiring the user to write each letter in a certain style—a requirement that dramatically reduces the patterns the software must recognize. But even with this simplification, pattern recognition must be supplemented by additional contextual information. How should the software recognize the handwritten figure:

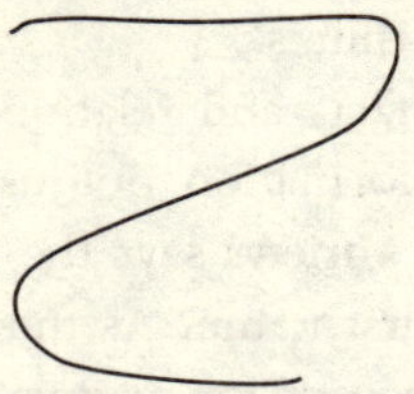

Without additional context, the software could narrow the meaning to two possibilities—the letter "z" or the number "2"—but it could not go further than that. To solve the problem, the Palm OS imposes a piece of contextual knowledge by dividing the writing area into two parts. If the character is written on the left side of the area, the software will process it as a letter. Written on the right side, the character will be processed as a number. Unlike the knowledge that people are not 1/4-inch tall, this knowledge is quite arbitrary. But without this context, the character's meaning is ambiguous.

The need for context means that present-day software can be programmed to recognize only relatively straightforward patterns—patterns that do not present serious perceptual problems or require vast amounts of contextual knowledge in order to be identified. ImageChecker is neural net software that scans digitized mammograms for patterns associ-

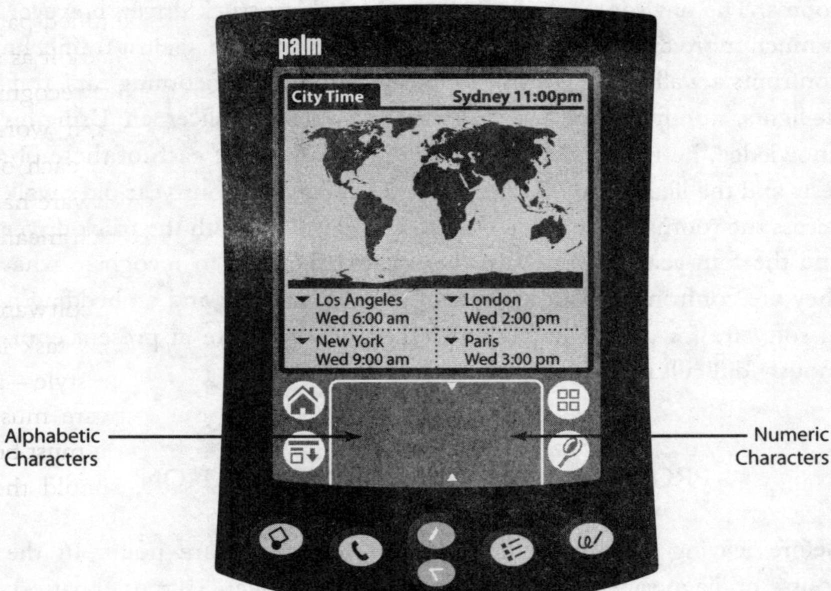

Figure 2.1. The Palm Pilot.

ated with cancer. As with all neural networks, ImageChecker must first be trained on previously analyzed mammograms to "learn" which visual patterns to flag.[16] Once trained, the software provides an effective complement to the radiologist's work. As one clinician describes it,

> 'The current [computer-aided detection] algorithms are extremely good at detecting suspicious calcium deposits, which is one of the signs of breast cancer, but they are not as good at detecting subtle masses. The radiologist tends to be a little better in that category.'[17]

With pattern recognition, as with rules-based software, there are ways to push back against these limits. The Roomba vacuum cleaner is an example of a new wave of robotics in which the software is designed around the general features of a room. When the Roomba is placed in a specific room, it does not have to be trained in advance but learns the pattern of a room piece by piece as it moves along the floor, sensing obstacles and open spaces.[18]

The Roomba's software exploits the common features shared by most rooms. The environment confronting the bakery truck driver, however, is much more diverse. As the driver makes his left turn against traffic, he confronts a wall of images and sounds generated by oncoming cars, traffic lights, storefronts, billboards, trees, and a traffic policeman. Using his knowledge, he must estimate the size and position of each of these objects and the likelihood that they pose a hazard. The four-year-old's walk across the room for the apple is almost as complex. Both the truck driver and the four-year-old girl have the schema required to recognize what they are confronting. But articulating this knowledge and embedding it in software for all but highly structured situations are at present enormously difficult tasks.

PROGRAMMING HUMAN INTERACTION

Before leaving pattern recognition consider one more point. In the course of diagnosing Harold's heart problem, Stephen Saltz used pattern recognition not once but twice: once to interpret the echocardiogram, but before that, to converse with his patient, Harold. We should not be surprised at this. Human interaction often involves exchanging complex information in ways that raise all the information-processing problems described in this chapter. These problems limit a computer's ability to interact with people.

We have seen that verbal information is processed in context (How do you interpret "BILL"?). This raises a central problem: when two people do not share the same context, the recipient of information may interpret it differently from how the conveyer intended. We encounter this problem all the time. A woman receives an email from a coworker: "This day has been so crazy that I'm going to jump out the window." Is the email a vent or a suicide note? Unless the woman knows the coworker well, she cannot say.

When the information involves sensitive topics, the exchange can be extremely complex because a recipient's context includes aroused emotions—powerful feelings with obscure connections to the situation at hand. (We return to emotions in chapter 5.)

When Stephen Saltz diagnoses a patient's illness, these problems arise frequently. A patient's initial description of symptoms may be imprecise ("I have this pain in my side") and Saltz may not understand what the patient means. Even worse, the patient may fear what Saltz will discover and so will talk about everything except the symptoms that worry him.

Good doctors learn to deal with these problems. They learn how to frame questions that elicit clarifying responses ("Is it a sharp pain or a dull pain? What times of the day does the pain occur? Does it occur after eating?"). They learn how to read the patient's body language—the avoidance of eye contact or the broken off sentence that indicates holding something back. They learn how to build patient confidence—spending time at the beginning of an appointment just listening to the patient without writing notes conveys a sense of caring. They learn that the most important moment in an appointment may come as the patient is walking out the door: "By the way, Doctor, I should have mentioned . . ."

Not all workplace conversations are as complex as those Saltz has with his patients. The purchase of an airline ticket, for instance, often can be accomplished using limited amounts of information: prices, dates, airports, seat availability, credit card number. Like the restricted information for the GE technician's work order, the customer's ticket request can be processed by rules and these rules power websites like Orbitz.com and Expedia.com. Just as ATMs capture rules-based parts of a teller's job, these sites capture rules-based parts of a travel agent's job. They cannot perform all travel-related tasks, but the tasks that they do perform are sufficient to sell $50 million in airline tickets per day.[19]

At the same time, conversations critical to effective teaching, managing, selling, and many other occupations require the transfer and interpretation of a broad range of information. In these cases, the possibility of exchanging information with a computer, rather than another human, is a long way off. We return to these issues in chapter 5.

SUBSTITUTION AND COMPLEMENTARY REVISITED

We began this chapter by asking why computers affect different jobs differently—why computers substituted for the jobs of the Liffe floor traders while complementing the diagnostic techniques of cardiologist

Processing Tasks
(listed in order of increasing complexity)

Conscious application of rules	Application of implicit rules that human observers can infer	Pattern recognition based on implicit rules that learning software can infer	Pattern recognition (rules cannot be inferred)
Examples			
Arithmetic	Mortgage underwriting	Detection of cancerous cell clusters in mammograms	A truck driver turning left against traffic; a doctor reading an echocardiogram

Figure 2.2. Varieties of Human Information Processing.

Stephen Saltz. The answer lies in the variety of ways that humans process information. As illustrated in figure 2.2, we can think of a spectrum of increasingly complex processing in which we move from tasks involving the application of specific rules (on the left) through tasks requiring pattern recognition (on the right).

Computers excel at the rapid application of rules. A task that can be fully described by rules is a strong candidate for computer substitution. By contrast, computers can recognize patterns only in fairly restricted situations—those that don't present complex perceptual problems and have only modest requirements for contextual knowledge. Jobs that require complex pattern recognition remain a largely human domain. But note how this description applies to two different kinds of jobs—jobs requiring extensive optical recognition and physical movement (the truck driver) and jobs requiring complex thought processes (Stephen Saltz diagnosing a patient). Computers cannot easily substitute for humans in these jobs but they can complement humans by providing large volumes of information at low cost—a GPS navigation system for the truck driver, an echocardiograph for Stephen Saltz.

Our next step is to apply this framework to understand how advances in computerization are affecting the distribution of jobs in the economy and the skills these jobs demand.

CHAPTER 3

How Computers Change Work and Pay

DESIGNING AIRPLANES

In November 1962 Boeing launched the 727, a 131-passenger jetliner designed to operate out of small airports with short runways. The roll-out completed an eighty-one-month development process during which more than 5,000 engineers worked with thousands of pounds of blueprints to design an aircraft that included more than 100,000 parts.[1] The airplane's complexity meant that no one person could guarantee the blueprints' internal consistency and so the second step in the design process was the construction of a full-scale model to ensure that the components fit—that proper space had been left for the aircraft's seats, hydraulic lines, air conditioning ducts, and other components.

When the model was completed and blueprints had been corrected, design engineers translated blueprint specifications into settings for stamping presses, turning lathes and the other machine tools that would fabricate the 727's parts. The translation resulted in many small errors and the parts often fit imperfectly. Assembly workers had to adjust the parts by hand, using metal shims to fill in small gaps. A manager familiar with the process estimated that a 727 weighing forty-four tons typically contained a half-ton of shims.

Thirty-two years later, in April 1994, Boeing rolled out the 777, a 305-passenger plane designed to carry passengers up to 6000 miles. Although much larger and more complex than the 727, the 777's development cycle was shorter by twenty-nine months. The explanation was no secret: the 777 was the first commercial jet to be completely designed using computers. Using CATIA, computer-assisted design and manufacturing software developed by the French engineering company Dassault Systèmes, engineers designed components on computer screens rather than on paper. The software's power was its ability to integrate individual views into a three-dimensional visualization. The virtual model substituted for a physical mock-up in checking plans for internal consistency. Once engineers had corrected the plans, CATIA produced the digital settings for the computer-numerically-controlled (CNC) machine tools that would fabricate the 777's parts.

Boeing purchased the CATIA system as part of an effort to pursue several competitive strategies. One was to compete better by increasing design speed. Being first to market confers an advantage in many industries but it is particularly important in civilian aircraft, where two large producers—Boeing and Airbus—vie for a limited number of orders. Boeing's adoption of CATIA eliminated the need for mock-up models and reduced the time required to correct plans and to set up machine tools. The result was a 36 percent reduction in the length of Boeing's development cycle.

A second competitive strategy facilitated by CATIA was improved product quality. The digital settings that CATIA produced for CNC machine tools made it possible to produce parts that fit together well and so the 777's assembly required far fewer hand adjustments and shims. According to Boeing, "[T]he first 777 was just .023 of an inch—about the thickness of a playing card—within perfect alignment while most airplane parts line up to within a half inch of each other."[2]

Since CATIA reduced design time, its use made it possible for Boeing to compete by offering product variety. It could provide configurations tailored to customers' specifications without long design delays.

The digital machine tool settings produced by CATIA facilitated another Boeing competitive strategy: the ability to outsource production with less regard to distance. In chapter 2, we saw how computerization made it possible to outsource call center work. Similarly, CATIA facilitated the outsourcing of blue-collar manufacturing work. Once CATIA produced the digital machine tool settings, the machine tools themselves could be located anywhere since Boeing knew the parts would fit when brought to a common assembly point. Boeing used this ability to locate production in Italy, the United Kingdom, Japan, and other countries, in part to attract foreign customers and in part to reduce production costs. (In retailing, a similar conquering of geography occurs as firms like Amazon.com and LandsEnd.com use single websites to reach widely dispersed customers and use computerized shipping to deliver orders in acceptably short times.[3])

None of these strategies was new. Fifty years ago Boeing wanted to bring high-quality planes to market as soon as possible and to tailor specifications to customers' preferences. What was new—what computers had changed—was the cost of pursuing the strategies. Fifty years ago, bringing aircraft to market sooner without compromising quality would have involved paying vast amounts of overtime. The adoption of computer-based design tools and computer-driven production tools dramatically lowered the cost of achieving these goals.

If we take a step back from aircraft production, we see how the Boeing-CATIA story illustrates a final computer-supported strategy—the creation of new, information-intensive products including CATIA itself, an important revenue source for Dassault Systèmes. CATIA, CDs, cell phones, DVDs, geo-positioning devices, the modern echocardiograph machine, the Eurex Trading network, complex financial derivatives, and the Palm Pilot are all successful products that computers have made possible.

WHY JOBS CHANGE

As the Boeing-CATIA example illustrates, computers change work through a three-step process. The first step occurred when Boeing purchased CATIA to pursue particular competitive strategies that were impractical without computers. To take advantage of CATIA's capabilities,

Boeing next had to reorganize work, using computers to substitute for humans in carrying out some tasks and to complement humans in carrying out others. In the process's final step, the reorganization of work changed both Boeing's job mix and the skills needed to do many jobs. Engineers now had to create designs on computer screens rather than drafting boards. The labor hours required to build a full-scale mock-up were no longer needed and the number of hours spent hand-fitting parts was sharply reduced. Some jobs that had been previously located in the United States were moved offshore.

The same three-step process characterizes almost every new application of computers. Firms adopt computers to gain a particular competitive advantage. Realizing computers' potential requires reorganizing work. As computers proliferate in the workplace, the jobs they create, destroy, and change are the byproduct of this work reorganization. Since computers are present in a large and growing number of American workplaces, they are catalyzing dramatic change in the nature of work. We turn to these changes.

FOUR WAYS TO THINK ABOUT WORK

When we ask how computers are changing work, we have several specifics in mind.

1. ***Employment***. With all the prophecies that computers would create mass unemployment, why didn't it happen?
2. ***The economy's mix of jobs***. As computers have substituted for humans in carrying out some tasks and complemented humans in tackling others, what kinds of jobs have grown in importance, and what kinds of jobs have declined?
3. ***Wages***. What are the wage trends for different kinds of workers, and what do these trends tell us the about the changing content of work?
4. ***Worker skills***. Which skills are of rising importance in the economy and which skills face diminishing demand? The answer to this question involves changes in the economy's mix of jobs but also the changing nature of work *within* jobs.

Employment

As this book goes to press, the economy continues in a post-bubble recession, but the current unemployment rate is nothing like the fear of mass unemployment expressed in the Ad Hoc Committee's 1964 memo to President Lyndon Johnson. Moreover, if we focus on the unemployment rate per se, we will miss the economy's strong job-creation performance as computer use soared.

When the Ad Hoc Committee drafted its memo, mainframe computers were a commercial reality and special-purpose computers—for example, computers that control machine tools—were on the horizon. Had computers created large-scale unemployment, we should have seen the first signs by the end of the 1960s. In fact, the opposite occurred. For much of the 1970s and 1980s, the labor force grew explosively as the largest baby-boom cohorts turned twenty-one and women of all ages moved into paid work. The fast growth in the number of potential workers meant that the number of jobs had to grow rapidly to keep unemployment from rising. In 1969, a boom year, unemployment stood at 3.5 percent. In 2000, another boom year, unemployment stood at 4.0 percent. In the intervening thirty-one years, the number of employed persons had grown from 83 million to 135 million—clearly not the picture the Ad Hoc Committee had expected.[4]

We have made reference to Herbert Simon's 1960 essay, "The Corporation: Will It Be Managed by Machines?" In this essay, Simon explained why predictions of mass unemployment would prove to be wrong. Borrowing from international trade theory, Simon invoked David Ricardo's historic principle of comparative advantage. Simon began from the premise that society can always find uses for additional output (consider today's unfulfilled demand for health care). Under this premise, computers and humans will both be used in producing this output, each in those tasks for which they have a comparative advantage. As Simon wrote:

> If computers are a thousand times faster than bookkeepers in doing arithmetic, but only one hundred times faster than stenographers in taking dictation, we shall expect the number of bookkeepers per thousand employees to decrease but the number of stenographers to increase. Similarly, if computers are a hundred

> times faster than executives in making investment decisions, but only ten times faster in handling employee grievances (the quality of the decisions being held constant), then computers will be employed in making investment decisions, while executives will be employed in handling grievances. (25)

Note that in Simon's examples (as in Ricardo's original formulation), computers are absolutely more efficient than humans in both tasks but employing humans is still worthwhile in tasks in which they have a *comparative* (that is, relative) advantage. As we know, our current situation is not this extreme since humans are absolutely more efficient than computers in understanding speech, interpreting visual images, and in a host of other activities requiring recognition of complex patterns. At the same time, Simon does not rule out that the adoption of computers may cause painful adjustments or that workers displaced by computers may regain employment only at lower wages, at least in the short run.

The story Simon describes has played out with many different technologies. When the combine harvester came into widespread use in the 1920s, it displaced manual labor and created substantial rural unemployment. Over the longer run, most farm workers became reemployed through either of two channels.

In the first channel, greater efficiency in agriculture meant that farm products could be sold at lower prices, and so consumers could increase the amounts they purchased. Workers were rehired to help produce the larger levels of output now demanded by consumers.

In the past twenty years, this channel has characterized "back-office" jobs in the securities industry. Consider the entry-level accountants who keep the books for mutual funds and compute the Net Asset Value per share (NAV) that appears in daily newspaper stock tables. Over two decades, the computerization of their job has allowed the average accountant to keep records for four mutual funds instead of one or two. Had the number of mutual funds stayed constant, the accountants' greater productivity would have meant fewer accounting jobs. But over the same period, the number of mutual funds expanded from 500 to 5,000 and the number of mutual fund accountants significantly increased. The growth in the number of mutual funds stemmed, in part, from the decline in the cost of running a mutual fund as computers lowered the costs of record keeping, trade execution, and other back-office functions.[5]

The second, more important channel of reemployment was the movement of displaced workers into other, expanding industries. In the first half of the twentieth century, large numbers of displaced agricultural workers moved into manufacturing jobs. Similarly, beginning in the 1970s, displaced manufacturing workers moved into service jobs. These moves can be painful and can involve significant cuts in pay and benefits, but they avoid long-term unemployment.[6]

Under both channels, the economy produces more goods and services per person. In the agricultural example, the mechanical harvester allows the same amount of farm product to be produced with fewer farm laborers. Depending on demand, the displaced laborers produce either additional farm products or additional output in the industries to which they moved. This additional output is no economists' fantasy. In 1947, the median U.S. family income stood at $20,400 (in year-2001 dollars).[7] By 1964, it had risen to $31,773. The growing purchasing power largely reflected increased output per worker stemming from technological improvements and a more educated workforce. Over the long run, we can pay ourselves only what we produce, and it was the higher output per worker that permitted family incomes to rise.

Today, median family income stands at about $51,000, and a significant fraction of recent income gains has been spent on computer-related products: cell phones, advanced medical treatments, CDs, DVDs, and so on. These purchases, in turn, increased employment in those occupations in which labor had a comparative advantage.

In sum, plenty of evidence supports Simon's argument that computerized work does not lead to mass unemployment. But Simon also made clear that computerization could sharply alter the economy's mix of jobs. We turn next to this topic.

The Mix of Jobs

How do computers affect the economy's job mix? Most predictions have fallen into one of two schools. The first is that computers will do low-level, routine work, so that people have to move into higher-skilled work to survive. The second is that computers will largely do high-level work, leaving most people no alternative but menial jobs.

Peter Drucker, the management theorist, has been an enthusiastic member of the first school. In Drucker's mind, computerization subsumes routine work, and so the real danger is a shortage of trained managers to direct what computers should do. Writer Jeremy Rifkin is a member of the second school. In *The End of Work*, Rifkin argues that the economy's requirements for high-level knowledge workers can never compensate for the number of jobs computers will eliminate. The result will be a large concentration of workers in low-level dead-end jobs. Apparent support for this prediction comes from the U.S. Bureau of Labor Statistics, which projects that food preparation and serving workers—a low-paying occupation requiring little training—will gain more jobs in the decade from 2000 to 2010 than any other occupation.[8]

In his 1960 essay Herbert Simon made a set of predictions about the job mix in a typical corporation in 1985. Simon's predictions were closer to Drucker's than to Rifkin's, but they were also highly nuanced. While Simon did not lay out an explicit cognitive framework, something like the framework discussed in chapter 2 was implicit in the predictions he made for a variety of occupational categories.

- Blue-collar workers: "There will be a few vestigial "workmen"—probably a smaller part of the total labor force than today—who will be part of in-line production, primarily doing tasks requiring relatively flexible eye-brain-hand coordination." (37)
- Machine maintenance workers (people we now call technicians): "There will be a substantial number of men whose task it is to keep the system operating by preventative and remedial maintenance." (37)
- Clerical workers: "The same kinds of technical developments that lead toward the automatic factory are bringing about an even more rapid revolution—and perhaps eventually a more complete one—in large-scale clerical operations. . . . We can conjecture that by 1985, the departments of a company concerned with major clerical functions—accounting, processing of customers' orders, inventory and production control, purchasing

and the like—will have reached an even higher level of automation than most factories." (26)

- Salespeople: "I have little basis for conjecture on this point. If we think that buying decisions are not going to be made much more objectively than they have in the past, then we might conclude the automation of the salesman's role will proceed less rapidly than the automation of many other jobs. If so, selling will account for a larger fraction of total employment." (37)
- Managers: "There will be a substantial number of men at professional levels, responsible for the design of product, for the design of productive process, and for general management. We have still not faced the question of how far automation will go in these areas, and hence we cannot say very firmly whether such occupations will be a larger or smaller part of the whole." (38)

Note how some of Simon's predictions made in 1960 run counter to predictions made by business analysts in the 1990s. Simon's emphasis on managers goes against the precepts of re-engineering in which information technology would eliminate layers of managers. His qualified emphasis on salespeople runs counter to predictions that e-commerce would dramatically reduce the number of salespeople.

Were Simon's predictions accurate? It is time to look at the numbers. To see what actually happened to occupations, we first present the 1969 occupational structure for adult workers (figure 3.1). Data for the figure come from the U.S. Census Bureau, which classifies workers into roughly 400 occupational titles, including the following: Managers [in] Marketing, Advertising, and Public Relations; Administrators [in] Education and Related Fields; Funeral Directors; and Buyers [in] Wholesale and Retail Trade, Except Farm Products. To make these data comprehensible, figure 3.1 groups the detailed occupational titles into seven broad categories arrayed from left to right in order of increasing average earnings.[9]

The category "Professional Occupations" in figure 3.1 includes teachers, ministers, doctors, engineers, and other white-collar jobs typically requiring college or post-college education. "Blue-Collar Workers" includes skilled craftsmen, assembly line workers, day laborers, and similar workers, most of whom work in industrial settings and have not com-

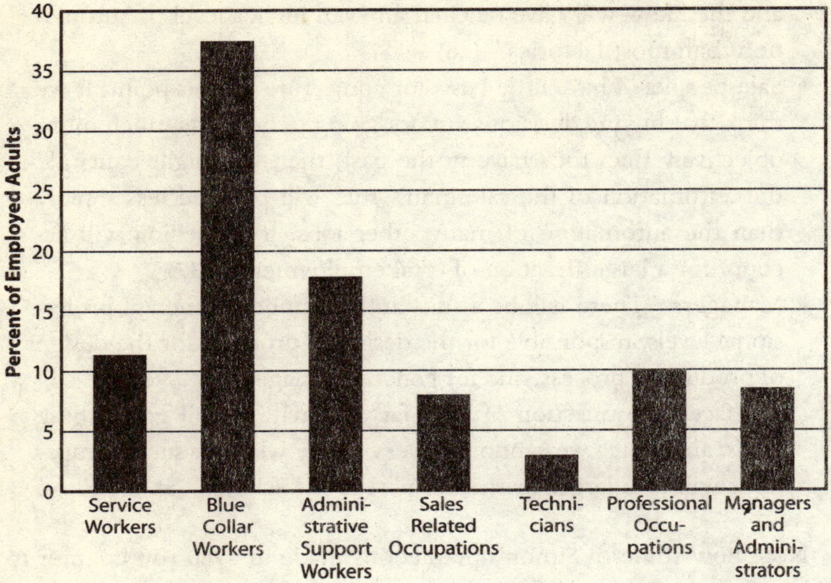

Figure 3.1. The Adult Occupational Distribution: 1969. Source: Authors' tabulations of data from the March 1970 Current Population Survey.

pleted college.[10] The category "Service Workers" includes janitors, cafeteria servers and waiters, policemen, firemen, childcare workers, and others who deal with people face to face; many of these jobs do not require a college degree (policemen are now an exception in many jurisdictions but were not so in 1969).

The variety of occupations in each category blurs the meaning of the category's average earnings. Service workers *on average* earn less than blue-collar workers, but the highest paid service workers—policeman and firemen—earn more than many blue-collar workers and many sales workers as well. Nonetheless, the figure gives a reasonable overview of the U.S. occupational structure.

Figure 3.2 shows how these occupational groupings changed in relative size between 1969 and 1999, a period when computers of all kinds permeated the economy. (We chose 1999 instead of a later year as the end point of our comparison in order to compare two business-cycle peak years.) Reading the figure from left to right, we learn the following:

- Service Workers grew modestly from 11.6 percent of all workers in 1969 to 13.9 percent in 1999.
- Blue Collar Workers and Administrative Support Workers both declined. Together, these two occupational groups employed 56 percent of all adult workers in 1969, falling to 39 percent of all adult workers in 1999.
- Sales Related Occupations ranging from McDonald's clerks to stockbrokers to real estate agents grew from 8 percent to 12 percent of all adults—from one adult worker in every twelve to one in every eight.[11]
- Technicians increased from 4.2 percent to 5.4 percent of all adult workers.
- Professional Occupations—engineers, teachers, scientists, lawyers—increased from 10 percent to 13 percent—from one worker in ten to one in eight.
- Managers and Administrators increased from 8 percent to 14 percent—from one adult worker in twelve to one in every seven.

This hollowing out of the occupational structure is broadly consistent with Simon's predictions including his general expectation of more "face-to-face interaction." With one exception, it is also consistent with Peter Drucker's view of the world—that the growth would be in jobs requiring more education. The exception is the modest growth of Service Workers at the bottom of the pay distribution.

To see why trends in Service Workers are difficult to predict, consider the statement that computers are best at doing routine jobs. In casual conversation, a security guard has a routine job: he or she walks the same beat every night looking for suspicious activity. But from a cognitive perspective, a security guard's job is exceedingly complex.[12] The core of the job—identifying suspicious activity—begins with the perception of large quantities of visual and aural information. This information must be processed using pattern recognition that requires substantial contextual knowledge. In casual conversation, "routine" means "repetitive." In soft-

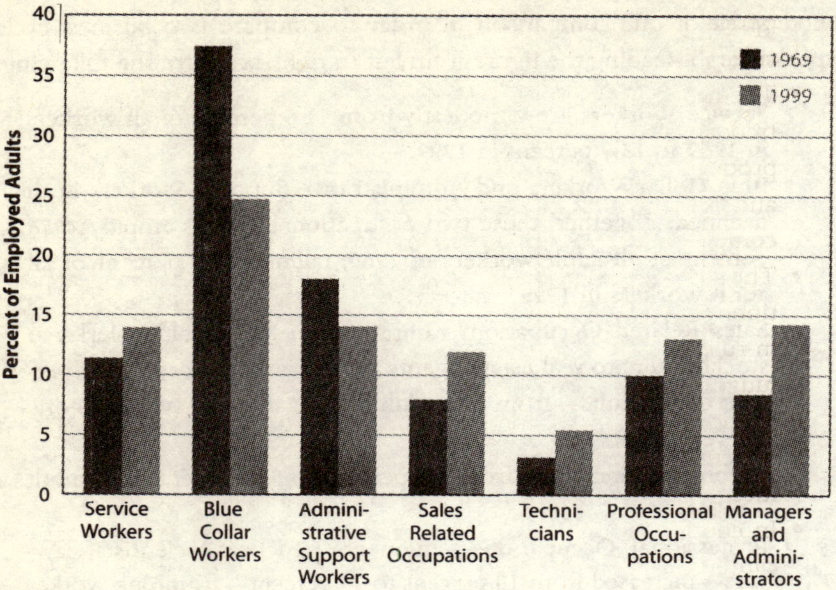

Figure 3.2. The Adult Occupational Distribution: 1969 and 1999. Source: Authors' tabulations of data from the March 1970 and March 2000 Current Population Surveys.

ware terms, however, "routine" means "expressible in rules." Determining whether a person is a potential burglar or a worker staying late is not easily encoded in rules.

A security guard is not paid well because most humans can do the job—that is, the potential supply of workers is large. But that does not mean the job is easy to program. The distinction between "easy for humans to do" and "easy to program computers to do" helps to explain why routine service workers—cafeteria workers, janitors—have not been replaced by computers and why the fraction of adults in service work has grown (see figure 3.2).[13]

More generally, the theory implicit in Simon's 1960 essay and explicit in chapter 2 provides a coherent story about why occupations changed as they did:

- The growing number of Service Workers (janitors, cafeteria workers, security guards) reflects the inability to describe human optical recognition and many physical movements in sets of rules.

- The growth of Sales Occupations (fast food clerks through bond traders) stems in part from the way that an increased flow of new products—driven by computers—increases the need for selling, and in part from the inability of rules to describe the exchange of complex information that salesmanship requires.
- The growth of Professional, Managerial and Technical occupations reflects the inability to express high end cognitive activities in rules: formulating and solving new problems, exercising good judgment in the face of uncertainty, creating new products and services. The competitive strategies listed earlier—strategies driven by computers—have increased demand for these activities.
- In contrast, many Blue Collar and Administrative Support jobs can be described in rules, and this accounts in large part for the decline in these two categories through both direct substitution and computer-assisted outsourcing.

The result is a picture in which the number of menial jobs is growing, but the general shift of occupations is toward higher-end jobs. While computers are not responsible for all of these changes, they do play a major role in bringing them about.[14]

Before leaving this picture, we have one loose end to consider—the Bureau of Labor Statistics (BLS) projection that food preparation and serving workers will be the occupation with the largest job growth over the next decade. How can this BLS projection square with the general shift of occupations toward higher-skilled jobs shown in figure 3.2?

The answer becomes clear once we put the projection into context. In the year 2000 there were more food preparation and food servers in the economy (about 2.2 million) than there were lawyers (681,000), doctors (598,000), or electrical engineers (450,000). But these head-to-head comparisons tell us little since food preparation and serving workers are counted under one occupational title while jobs requiring significant education tend to be divided into many occupations (e.g., electrical engineering is one of sixteen major engineering occupations classified in BLS statistics).

The shift that Jeremy Rifkin feared, a "deskilled" occupational structure, requires that the *total* number of low-skilled jobs (janitors plus security guards plus food preparation and service workers, etc.) increases more than the *total* number of higher-skilled jobs (lawyers plus doctors plus electrical engineers plus mechanical engineers, and so on). These totals are the kind of occupational categories displayed in figure 3.2, where the food preparation and service workers are included in Service Occupations. Once we move from individual job titles to occupational categories, the evidence of deskilling disappears. Between 1969 and 1999, the number of adults employed as Service Workers grew from 11.6 percent to 13.9 percent of the adult work force, but Managers, Administrators, Professional Workers, and Technicians taken together—the highest paid categories—grew from 23 percent to 33 percent.

The Distribution of Wages

In a healthy economy, demands for different kinds of workers are changing all the time—so quickly that it is easy for specific kinds of workers to find themselves in shortage or surplus. In the labor market, as in any other competitive market, the best indicators of shortages and surpluses are changes in prices—in this case, wages. When workers with particular attributes are in surplus, their real wages (net of inflation) fall. Real wages rise for workers in shortage. For the period we are examining, the best wage data comes from the decennial U.S. Census and its companion survey, the monthly Current Population Survey. Based on these data, figures 3.3 and 3.4 show trends over the period 1973–2001 in the average wages of male and female workers with different educational attainments.

In 1996 the average real wage of male college graduates was almost identical to its value in 1973, an indication that demand kept up with the supply of college-educated workers. Then in the strong economy of the late 1990s, the real wage of male college graduates grew markedly. In contrast, the average real wage of male high school graduates fell by almost \$3.00 per hour between 1973 and 1996, and the average wage of male dropouts fell by almost \$4.00 per hour during this period. While the strong economy of the late 1990s allowed these groups to recover some

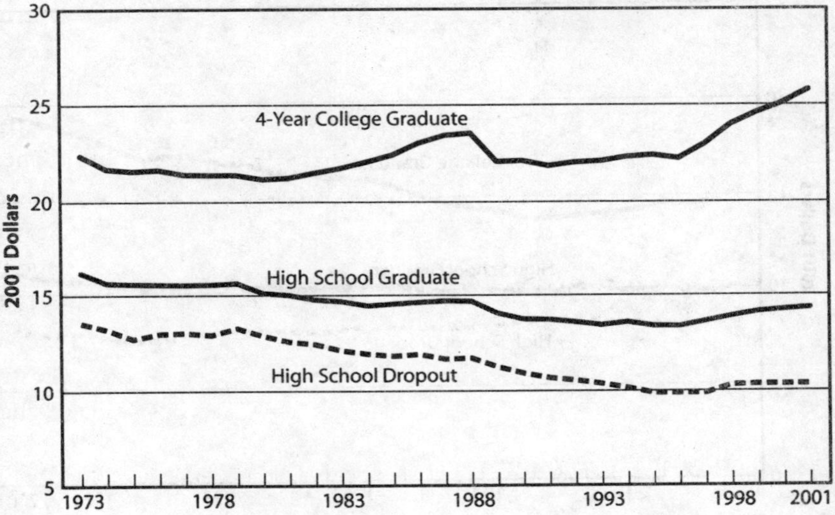

Figure 3.3. Real Hourly Wage Trends for Males 1973–2001, by education group. Source: Data from Current Population Surveys as reported on the Economic Policy Institute Website: http://www.epinet.org/datazone/02/ed_wages_m_2_18r.pdf.

part of the earnings decline, hourly wages in 2001 were still markedly below 1973 wages for these groups.

The pattern of wage stability and recent wage growth among college graduates and long-run wage decline among high school graduates could have come from changes in the demand for workers with different educational attainments or from changes in their supply. The data point to changes in demand. During this period, the number of male college graduates was growing *faster* than the number of male high school graduates and dropouts. Had demand been stable, the faster growing group would have experienced declining wages. That, of course, is not what happened—real wages of male college graduates rose in the two decades after 1980. The changing occupational structure was creating new demand for college graduates that outstripped their fast-growing supply. Applying the same logic, the real wages of male high school graduates and male dropouts were falling because demand for these workers was growing even more slowly than their slow-growing supply.[15]

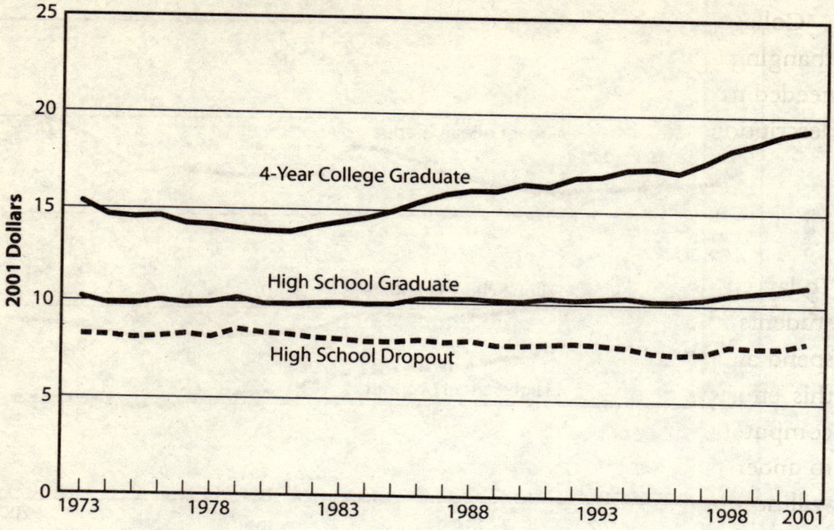

Figure 3.4. Real Hourly Wage Trends for Females 1973–2001, by education group. Source: Data from Current Population Surveys as reported on the Economic Policy Institute Website: http://www.epinet.org/datazone/02/ed_wages_w_2_19r.pdf.

Women's wages tell a broadly similar story. As with men, the number of employed female college graduates grew faster during these years than the number of employed female high school graduates and dropouts. Yet as shown in figure 3.4, the average wage of female college graduates increased quite sharply while the average wage of female high school graduates and school dropouts did not grow.

We are beginning to fill in the blanks about how computers are changing work. On the labor market's demand side, the share of menial jobs has increased modestly, but the largest job growth has been in occupations requiring significant education. On the labor market's supply side, the number of college graduates has been growing faster than the number of high school graduates and dropouts. Yet the rising wages of college graduates indicate demand is outstripping their supply. Conversely, the declining wages of male high school graduates and dropouts, despite the slow growth of these groups, indicate they will end up in jobs that no longer pay enough to support families.

College graduates have fared better than high school graduates in the changing U.S. labor market because they are more likely to have the skills needed to do the tasks that are part of high-wage jobs. We turn now to a description of these tasks.

Worker Skills and the New Nature of Work

Today virtually all public schools operate under mandates to prepare all students to master skills defined in state standards. Private corporations spend an average of $800 per employee on training each year.[16] Much of this effort is devoted to preparing people to work productively in the computerized workplace. If the effort is to make sense, the nation needs to understand what tasks humans will do at their work and the skills they will need to carry out these tasks effectively.

We already have some answers. We have established that computers have a comparative advantage over people in carrying out tasks requiring the execution of rules, but people have the comparative advantage in recognizing complex patterns. We have also seen how complex pattern recognition is critical in two quite different kinds of tasks—optical recognition and physical movement (security guards, Simon's "few vestigial 'workmen'") and tasks involving higher-order cognitive skills. As a next step we can usefully divide these higher order tasks into two broad groups. The first are tasks that involve solving new problems—problems that cannot be solved by applying well-understood rules. The second are tasks that require explanation, negotiation, persuasion, and other forms of intense human interaction. We will call these two sets of tasks, respectively, tasks requiring expert thinking and tasks requiring complex communication.

In joint work with David Autor of MIT's Department of Economics, we have shown that tasks requiring expert thinking and complex communication are two of five broad kinds of tasks carried out by the U.S. labor force:[17]

- Expert thinking: solving problems for which there are no rule-based solutions. Examples include diagnosing the illness of a patient whose symptoms seem strange, creating a good tasting dish from the ingredients that are fresh in the market that morning, repairing an auto that does not run well but that the computer diagnostics indicate has no problem. By definition, these are not tasks that computers can be programmed to do. While computers cannot substitute for humans in these tasks, they can complement humans in performing them by making information more readily available.

- Complex communication: interacting with humans to acquire information, to explain it, or to persuade others of its implications for action. Examples include a manager motivating the people whose work she supervises, a biology teacher explaining how cells divide, an engineer describing why a new design for a DVD player is an advance over previous designs.
- Routine cognitive tasks: mental tasks that are well described by logical rules. Examples include maintaining expense reports, filing new information provided by insurance customers, and evaluating applications for mortgages. Because these tasks can be accomplished by following a set of rules, they are prime candidates for computerization.
- Routine manual tasks: physical tasks that can be well described using rules. Examples include installing windshields on new vehicles in automobile assembly plants, and counting and packaging pills into containers in pharmaceutical firms. Since these tasks can be defined in terms of a set of movements to be carried out over and over in exactly the same way, they are also candidates for computerization.
- Nonroutine manual tasks: physical tasks that cannot be well described as following a set of If-Then-Do rules because they require optical recognition and fine muscle control that have proven extremely difficult for computers to carry out. Examples include driving a truck, cleaning a building, and setting gems in engagement rings. Computers do not complement human effort in carrying out most such tasks. As a result, computerization should have little effect on the percentage of the work force engaged in these tasks.

Earlier in this chapter, we saw how the nation's occupational distribution has changed in the period from 1969 to 1999. In the same way, we can look for changes in the nature of the tasks that comprise this work. While the Census does not ask about the content of work, a second survey does—the U.S. Department of Labor's Dictionary of Occupational Titles (DOT).

The DOT is a compilation of 12,000 detailed occupational descriptions, each containing professional observers' ratings of the training time required for the occupation, the occupation's physical and cognitive requirements, and other characteristics. Because an occupation's details can vary across work sites, each occupation is rated across many workers in multiple sites and the DOT provides an average of the ratings.

The DOT offers far from perfect data. Updates are infrequent, and so it is difficult to track changes in tasks that occur within occupations. Nonetheless, the DOT allows an approximate translation of changes in the economy's distribution of occupations into changes in the kind of tasks that people perform in the workplace.[18] Figure 3.5 displays the trend for each of these five types of tasks. Each trend reflects changes in the numbers of people employed in occupations emphasizing that task. To facilitate comparisons, the importance of each task in the U.S. economy is set to zero in 1969, our baseline year. The value in each subsequent year represents the percentile change in the importance of each type of task in the economy.[19]

A quick look at the figure shows that, consistent with our expectations, tasks requiring pattern recognition grew in frequency while rules-based tasks declined. Complex communication is important in management, teaching, and sales occupations among others. As the occupational structure evolved toward these particular occupations, the frequency of tasks requiring complex communication grew steadily during the 1970s, 1980s, and 1990s. The frequency of tasks requiring expert thinking—tasks that involved solving new problems—followed a similar growth path.

For rules-based tasks where computers can substitute for humans, the picture is one of decline. The share of the labor force employed in occupations that emphasized routine cognitive tasks remained quite steady during the 1970s and then declined quite precipitously over the next two

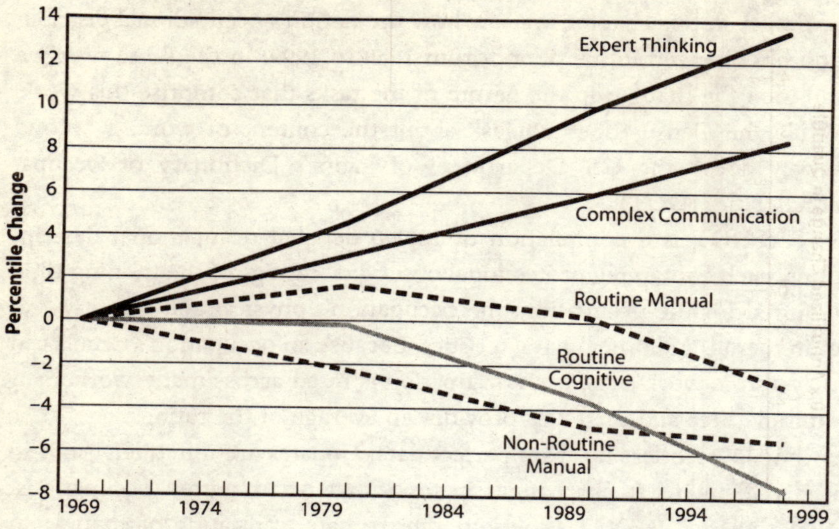

Figure 3.5. Economy-Wide Measures of Routine and Non-Routine Task Input: 1969–98 (1969 = 0). Revised version of figure from David Autor, Frank Levy, and Richard J. Murnane, "The Skill Content of Recent Technological Change: An Empirical Exploration," *Quarterly Journal of Economics* 118 (November 2003): 4.

decades. The pattern for routine manual tasks—tasks that might be subsumed by automation—is roughly similar: a slight rise during the 1970s and a steady decline in the subsequent two decades. The share of the labor force working in occupations that emphasize nonroutine manual tasks declined throughout the period. This reflects in part the movement of manufacturing jobs offshore.

The data in figures 3.2 (occupations) and 3.5 (tasks) are consistent with our description of computers' economic impacts. But this correlation does not prove causation—the trend in both figures could have been caused by other factors. To make a stronger case, we must increase the level of detail to look at changes within industries. If our argument is right—if the adoption of computers shifts work away from routine tasks and toward tasks requiring expert thinking and complex communication—it should be observable when we look within industries. Specifically, we can ask: are those industries that invested most heavily in computers the industries where we see the greatest changes in task structure?

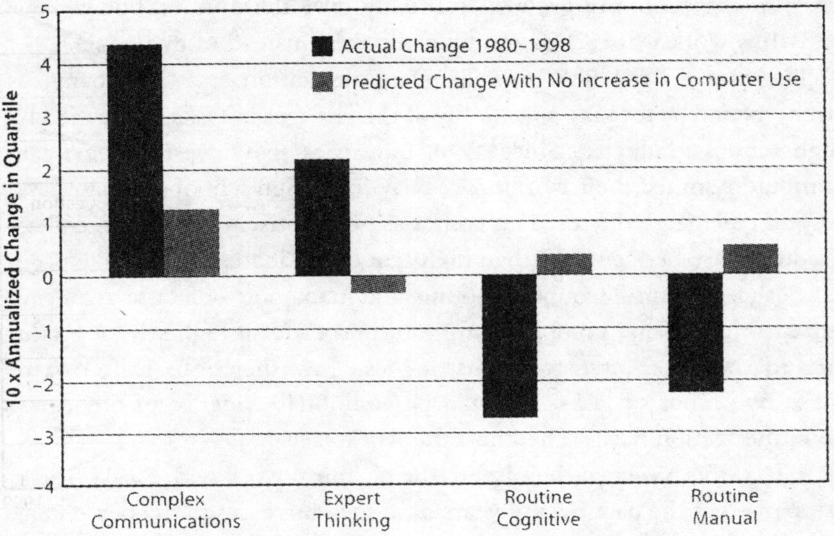

Figure 3.6. Within-Industry Changes in Task Frequency Between 1980 and 1998 (left bars) and Predicted Changes in Task Frequency Had There Been No Increase in Computer Use (right bars). Revised version of figure from David Autor, Frank Levy, and Richard J. Murnane, "The Skill Content of Recent Technological Change: An Empirical Exploration," *Quarterly Journal of Economics* 118 (November 2003): 4.

The answer is yes. In figure 3.6 the left of each pair of bars describes the average change in task frequency within industries over the period 1980 to 1998.[20] The height of the right bar in each pair is an estimate of the change in task frequency that would have occurred had there been no increase in computer use. A comparison of the bars in each pair illustrates that changes in task frequency have been concentrated in the industries experiencing the most rapid increases in computer use. This pattern is particularly striking for routine cognitive tasks. The percentage of the labor force employed in jobs that consisted primarily of carrying out routine cognitive tasks declined substantially over these years. The figure shows that in the absence of changes in computer use, the estimated percentage of the labor force working at routine cognitive tasks would have increased. The amount of routine information processing taking place in the economy grew substantially over these years, but increasingly this work was carried out by computers instead of by people.[21]

The case for the link between computerization and task change is strengthened by looking specifically at the changes in tasks performed by high school graduates. Since 1970, industries that invested heavily in computers shifted their workforces away from high school graduates and toward college graduates. This comes as no surprise. On average, college graduates are better suited than high school graduates for jobs like product design, technical trouble shooting, and managing—all tasks requiring expert thinking and complex communication. But if high school graduates in computer-intensive industries also saw their jobs shift toward these two kinds of tasks, it would be additional evidence of how deep computerization has reached into the workplace.

In fact, this has been the case. In the technical work with David Autor, we show that the past twenty years have seen increases in the percentage of high school graduates working at jobs that emphasize complex communication and substantial declines in the percentages of high school graduates working at jobs that emphasized routine cognitive or routine manual tasks. Consistent with our theory, these changes were concentrated in industries that experienced the greatest growth in computer usage.

WHY TASK CHANGES ARE ACTUALLY LARGER

While figure 3.5 displays large changes over the past thirty years in the tasks carried out by U.S. workers, the figure actually understates the changes that have taken place. Because the task content data from the Dictionary of Occupational Titles are updated infrequently, figure 3.5 displays only task changes resulting from shifts in the economy's mix of jobs. It does not reflect task changes that occur *within* jobs, but hundreds of examples show that task changes within jobs have been quite large.

Consider two examples, beginning with exceptions processing at Cabot Bank. Cabot Bank is a large, New England retail bank.[22] Ten years ago, each exceptions processing clerk in the bank's back offices worked with paper checks and handled a single kind of exception—say, overdrafts.

Within the customer's account, the overdraft might be part of a more complicated set of transactions, but this was not the clerk's concern. The unit's manager described the work as "checking your brains at the door."

Today exceptions clerks work with digitized images of checks and handle all exceptions in an account—overdrafts, stop payments, address changes, and so on—as they reconstruct what a customer was actually trying to do. If they want to advance, they are also expected to make suggestions to improve department operations. The job now requires both greater skills and more initiative. (We tell the full story of Cabot Bank in chapter 4.)

The job of stockbroker has changed in similar ways. Twenty years ago, most stockbrokers provided customers with buy and sell recommendations, company research, and general conversation. Advising customers on other financial issues—the best way to save for a child's education—was beyond their job. Stockbrokers were paid a substantial commission on each customer trade. The commission was a "bundled" price that covered the cost of the trade as well as the cost of the research and conversation time.

By the late 1990s, web-based trading through firms like E*TRADE threatened to undermine this arrangement. A customer could talk to a broker but then avoid the commission by trading on-line. Customers could download on-line research as well. Brokers have increasingly adopted a two-part response. They have changed their pricing so that they are paid a percentage of customer assets under management rather than a per trade commission. And consistent with our argument here, they have expanded what they do to include financial planning advice—retirement planning, college savings planning, and similar services not easily provided over the web—changes that require more knowledge and insight.

TASKS AND SKILLS

In this chapter we have provided a variety of evidence showing how computerization has altered the tasks that American workers perform in their jobs. Declining portions of the labor force are engaged in jobs that consist primarily of routine cognitive work and routine manual work—the types of tasks that are easiest to program computers to do. Growing proportions of the nation's labor force are engaged in jobs that emphasize expert thinking or complex communication—tasks that computers cannot do.

If the set of products and services produced in the economy did not change, there would be less and less good work for humans to do as advances in computerization increased the possibilities for substitution. Such a trend, however, would run directly counter to the profit motive. A task, once computerized, is potentially easy to replicate and so invites intense competition. The response to the competition is a constant drive to use advances in computer technology to develop new products and services—cell phones, DVDs, broad-band Internet, computer-assisted surgery, financial derivatives, sensors in cars—the list is endless. This drive to develop, produce, and market new products relies on the human ability to manage and solve analytical problems and communicate new information, and so it keeps expert thinking and complex communication in strong demand.

In the next two chapters we explain expert thinking and complex communication in greater detail, and describe the skills humans need to succeed in these tasks that constitute the good jobs in a rapidly computerizing economy.

II

THE SKILLS EMPLOYERS VALUE

CHAPTER 4

Expert Thinking

JUST SOMETHING YOU KNOW

Dennis LaGrand is a senior service technician at Medford Orbit, a new car dealership in Medford, Massachusetts.[1] Like most auto technicians today, he relies heavily on computers. He uses computerized diagnostic equipment. He reads on-line factory service bulletins. He relies on in-car flash memory chips that record episodic events.

The shop's diagnostic computer uses rules-based software and it complements the rules-based diagnostics that make up most of shop repair manuals. A nonworking rear windshield wiper in an SUV has several potential causes: a bad on-off switch, a burned-out wiper motor, a break in a circuit. Because these elements are linked systematically through the wiring harness, Dennis can use a hand-held computer and apply If-Then-Do tests to locate the failure. But not all problems can be solved in this way.

In late fall of 1998, a customer brought in a two-seater sports car that suffered from weak acceleration. Like the windshield wiper problem, weak acceleration has many potential causes. In this case, the customer reported that the car's automatic transmission was slipping.

Dennis, like other experienced technicians, listened to the customer's symptom description but did his own diagnosis. He took the car for a test drive. Ten minutes later, he was back in the garage, driving into his repair bay. As he got out of the car, he said, "The transmission is fine. The problem is that the engine is missing [i.e., the sparkplugs are misfiring]."

Dennis's diagnosis involved processing tactile information from the car's feel on the road and aural information from the sound of its engine. He did not consciously apply rules. From his perspective it was "just something you know." From a cognitive scientist's perspective, it was pattern recognition.

FINE DISTINCTIONS

A cognitive scientist would also note that Dennis's diagnosis differed from the customer's. This difference illustrates one aspect of expert thinking: experts recognize meaningful patterns of information that are not noticed by novices.

Recall Julio Kaplan, the international chess master in Stewart Dreyfus's experiment, who won at speed chess while keeping a running total of digits being read to him (chapter 2). Kaplan appeared to play—and win—by instantaneously recognizing patterns of pieces on the board. An earlier chess-based experiment reinforces the interpretation.

In the 1960s, Andreas deGroot had chess players of three different skill-levels look for a few seconds at configurations of pieces on a chess board projected on a screen. The images were then removed and the players were asked to reproduce the arrangements they had seen. When the configuration represented a set of positions that could arise in a game—an arrangement an experienced chess player would have thought about—grandmasters correctly reproduced the positions of twenty to twenty-five pieces. Good players below the rank of master reproduced the positions of fifteen or sixteen pieces, while novice players reproduced the positions of five or six.

The grandmasters' strong performance was consistent with pattern recognition, but it could have been attributed to something simpler—the grandmasters' strong visual perception. To settle the question, deGroot ran a second version of the experiment in which the pieces were arranged randomly, resulting in positions no player would have seen in a game. In this second version of the experiment, grandmasters, good players, and novices all reproduced the locations of five or six pieces. In other words, grandmasters and good players could quickly recognize and reproduce only those board patterns they had encountered and studied.[2]

The reliance of expert thinking on pattern recognition is no surprise—we have already defined the concept in terms of such recognition (chapter 3). Dennis LaGrand diagnosing the sports car's problem, a wine expert distinguishing among vintages, a lawyer seeing parallels between cases, Stephen Saltz reading Harold's echocardiogram, a carpenter recognizing the need for an extra-thick beam—the list is endless. This fine-grained recognition can be an end in itself, but it can also serve as an important complement to rules-based reasoning.

Consider a mechanical engineer confronting an unusual structural problem. Once she has the problem modeled mathematically, she likely knows the rules-based procedure to arrive at the answer. But deciding how to model the problem—choosing the best mathematical representation—is typically a problem of pattern recognition. Our use of computers reflects a similar division of labor. A rules-based Excel spreadsheet is efficient, but depends on our assigning it only those problems we know it can handle. Depending on the occupation, the expert may process information from words, tone of voice, touch, taste, or other sources. The common thread of expertise is the ability to recognize patterns that others do not see.

We can ask whether pattern recognition has to be so important. While Dennis's solution might not be fully articulated in rules, couldn't it be documented and indexed in a way that provides rules to new technicians?[3] In cognitive terms, could problem documentation support the case-based information processing described earlier, in which people solve new problems by drawing analogies to previously solved problems (chapter 2)?

Many organizations devote substantial effort to this type of documentation. We describe the incentive issues these efforts raise, at the end of this chapter. For the present, we can say that proper documentation can often give a technician a running start, but neither rules nor cases can fully convey the tacit knowledge that an experienced technician requires.

A thoughtful analysis of this problem was given by Julian Orr, an anthropologist who, before starting graduate school, worked as a Xerox service representative. Orr wrote his doctoral dissertation on the service rep's job. Xerox service reps repair large, complex copying machines. As explained by John Seely Brown and Paul Duguid, Orr's reps often function in a world of uncertainty because each machine is different:

> For each [machine] inevitably reflects the age and condition of its parts, the particulars and patterns of use, as well as the distinctive influences of the environment in which it sits—hot, cold, damp, dry, clean, dusty, secluded, in traffic, and so forth. . . . So, while everyone else assumes each machine is like the next, a rep knows each by its peculiarities and has to sort out general failings from particular ones. All this undirected machine behavior inevitably undermines the very premise of directive documentation [i.e., rules]. . . .
>
> The reps' real difficulties arose, however, not simply because the documentation had lapses. They arose more problematically because it told them what to do, but not why. It gave instructions, but it didn't explain. So when machines did something unpredicted, reps found themselves not just off the map, but there without a compass or tools for bushwhacking. At this point, reps needed to bridge the gap between the limits of prediction and reality. In short they needed to make some sense of the machine in order to fix it. Directive documentation, however, wasn't designed for sense making. It was designed for rule following.[4]

Auto repair poses the same cognitive problems. The service manager at Medford Orbit described a young, newly hired technician. "He graduated from this Orbit-sponsored training program. It's a good program and he did very well on all the tests. But he can't fix a doll carriage." True to the description, the young technician frequently asked other technicians for help.

The process by which doctors diagnose patients frequently relies on pattern recognition in similar ways. Jeff Silver, an internist, described the process of diagnosing the source of a dull pain that an older woman had been experiencing for the past four weeks:

> It was an upper stomach pain. She had a gassiness, a fullness. It got worse after eating. There was some chest discomfort, no trouble breathing. No heart palpitations. Some loose stool but no sign of blood in the stool. No fever or chills. Alka Seltzer gave her a little relief but it was temporary.
>
> Her medical history: she had high blood pressure, she was diabetic and overweight. She had an allergy to sulfa drugs. No family history of GI [gastro-intestinal] problems. She was taking medication for blood pressure and two medications for diabetes, neither of which was known to cause problems.

Note the wide range of patient information with which Silver began. Based on his understanding of the information, he did a physical exam that covered generic factors—blood pressure, heart rate—but also looked for certain symptoms and family history. He was now at the stage of narrowing down possibilities:

> I checked the stomach. She had a soft abdomen. In the epigastric region, there was no tenderness in the liver or spleen, no enlarged liver. No rebound in the abdomen, no resistance suggesting something was broken.

At this point, Silver concluded that there were two likely diagnoses: gastritis, perhaps a peptic ulcer problem, or a gall bladder problem. He would choose one of the diagnoses and begin a treatment plan that he would monitor to see if his diagnosis was correct.

A quarter century ago, Marsden Blois described this diagnostic process using a funnel-shaped diagram (see figure 4.1), in which a doctor begins with a broad set of information and narrows the range of possible explanations until reaching a specific conclusion.[5]

As Blois argued, computer-based tools are most useful toward the end of the process—the right-hand side of figure 4.1—where the doctor has narrowed the range of diagnoses and the remaining possibilities can be evaluated using rules. At the start of a process, potentially relevant information can be so diffuse—the symptoms, family history, current medications and their possible interactions—that rules would be too complex to formulate. It is like the truck driver's problem, bringing large quantities

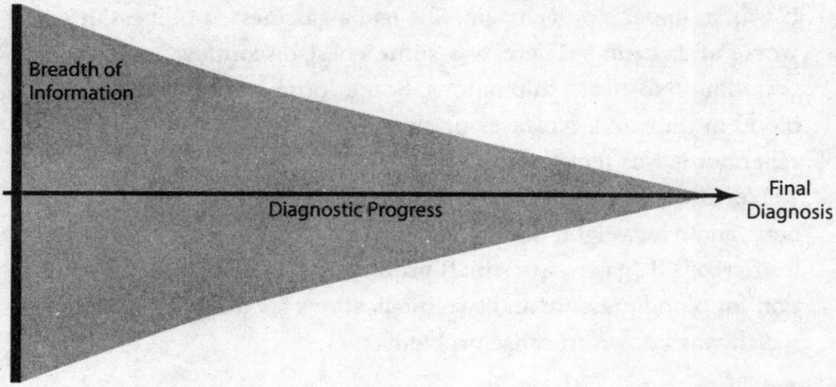

Figure 4.1. The Cognitive Span Required during Diagnosis. Source: Blois 1980, p. 193 (see note 5).

of knowledge to bear as he makes sense of what he sees while making a left turn across traffic (chapter 2). It is a task humans can perform but we cannot describe how we perform it.

SCHEMA

When Dennis LaGrand diagnosed the misfiring spark plugs, he had substantially narrowed the range of explanations for the car's problem but had not yet solved it. A sparkplug can misfire for many reasons—carbon buildup on the electrode, a problem in the engine's distributor, dirt in the car's fuel system. At the outset, Dennis considered only two of these possibilities.

"When the engine is missing, the first place you look is the plugs and the wires."[6] He began to disconnect the spark plug wires from the spark plugs to check them more carefully. The spark plugs sit in individual wells molded into the valve covers, the metal shells that sit on top of the engine. As Dennis felt the first spark plug, he realized the spark plug's well contained collected oil. The oil had rotted out the rubber shield that covers the end of the sparkplug wire that connects to the spark plug. Feeling the oil, Dennis knew there was a leak in the valve cover gasket that sits between the valve cover and the rest of the engine. The damaged gasket was leaking oil that collected in the spark plug wells, intermittently shorting out the plugs and causing the misfiring.

Dennis's explanation for how he was able to move quickly from the diagnosis to the solution illustrates a second aspect of expert thinking: experts have acquired a great deal of content knowledge that is organized in schemas that reflect a deep understanding of their subject matter.

The first part of the point seems obvious—if you don't know many facts about a subject, you are hard pressed to be an expert. But there was a time in computer science when this wasn't so clear. In the early days of expert system software—problem-solving software—designers, including Herbert Simon, were impressed by a human's ability to make at least some progress on virtually any problem. This observation led to a search for general strategies that could be applied to a wide variety of problems. Over time, designers came to realize that while humans made some progress on almost any problem, they made real progress only on those problems that they knew a lot about. As a result, expert systems became much more specialized, incorporating as many facts as possible in a specific domain—for example, facts about possible sources of a bloodstream infection, the kind of expert system that might lie at the narrow end of Marsden Blois's funnel (figure 4.1).[7]

But expertise requires more than facts. It requires understanding how the facts are linked together, how things actually work. These relationships allow a person to generalize from a specific case to a class of problems. Psychologists call these structures schemas—mental structures that represent concepts, like spark plugs and wires, and the relationships that connect them.

The difference between isolated facts and the organization of knowledge into schemas is nicely illustrated by two students' responses to a short oral quiz.

Student 1

Q. What was the date of battle of the Spanish Armada?

A. 1588.

Q. How do you know this?

A. It was one of the dates I memorized for the exam.

Q. Why is the event important?
A: I don't know.

Student 2

Q. What was the date of the battle of the Spanish Armada?
A. It must have been around 1590.
Q. How do you know this?
A. I know the English began to settle in Virginia just after 1600, although I'm not sure of the exact date. They wouldn't have dared start overseas explorations if Spain still had control of the seas. It would have taken a little while to get expeditions organized, so England must have gained naval supremacy somewhere in the late 1500s.
Q. Why is the event important?
A. It marks a turning point in the relative importance of England and Spain as European powers and colonizers of the New World.[8]

The second student had organized historical knowledge around patterns of causality. Dennis had linked misfiring spark plugs, oil in the spark plug wells, and leaking valve covers in a similar way. And Julio Kaplan had linked each board pattern he recognized to the next appropriate series of moves.

We can think of these schemas as equivalent to an engineering "work-around"—mental fixes to overcome a person's cognitive limits. Within the brain, our long-term memory has enormous capacity to store information. But our working memory—the information we can consciously consider at any instant—is quite small. This limit came to popular attention in George Miller's article, "The Magic Number Seven Plus or Minus Two."[9] Miller observed that we can hold no more than about seven random digits in our head at one time, but he also noted that we can recall more digits when the digits have been learned in patterns—1492, 1776, 1812, 1941. Roughly speaking, it takes only a little less working memory to hold the random digit 6 than it does to hold 1492, four digits we have linked with each other and with Columbus's voyage to America.

When we are looking for solutions, working memory acts like a spotlight, illuminating one small part of long-term memory and then another.[10] Without the efficient linking of facts in schema, the spotlight could wander endlessly before locating a good answer. It was this organization of knowledge that the young Medford Orbit technician ("He couldn't fix a doll carriage") had not mastered.

The need for organized knowledge appears in virtually all problem solving, including the creation of a menu. Tom and Rozann Buckner own and operate L'Epicureo, a restaurant on Federal Hill in Providence, Rhode Island. They have cooked together for more than twenty years. Before opening the restaurant, they had sold their own prepared foods in Rozann's father's butcher store, which had occupied the site where the restaurant now sits. Like most professionals, the Buckners rely on computers in their daily work: to send orders to the kitchen while keeping track of customers' bills, to keep inventory records, to process supply orders, and to store successful recipes. But the cognitive work of creating new recipes is substantially different from retrieving existing recipes.

On a Friday night in January 2002, L'Epicureo had offered a special of pasta shells and several kinds of mushrooms baked in a tomato/cream sauce. Tom described the creation of the dish:

> Every morning, I get a fax from my distributors saying what they have that's good. The previous morning I got a fax saying that they had in some great porcini mushrooms, so Rozann and I started talking back and forth about what we could do with that. At first, I said a plain cream sauce, but that was too bland. In the end we used a mix of two sauces—the pink sauce we used to sell frozen and the penne vodka sauce. We eliminated the nutmeg from the pink sauce and we eliminated the vodka from the penne vodka sauce.

Why did he combine two sauces?

> I wanted the brightness of the tomato to cut the cream in the pink sauce but if I had used too many chunks of tomatoes, the skins and pieces would have made the dish too coarse.

Why did he use shells in the dish?

> If I had chosen penne for the pasta, it would have died on the bottom of the dish when it was baked. I needed something that would stand up. So I used shells and they had the advantage of getting

> crisped around the edges, which is a nice touch. A pasta like cappeletti is popular, but you can't bake that dish with cappeletti because it would all stick together.
>
> So we cooked the dish and tasted it, served it to the staff—everyone agreed it was great—it didn't need any correction—so we put it on the menu.

In this dish, creation came quickly and reflected the couple's organized knowledge of the ways in which ingredients support and conflict with each other—the "things we know." The knowledge involves taste, texture, and color. Without it, creating each new dish would require a grueling process of trial and error. As in the case of the automobile diagnoses, a dish once created can be written down in the rules of a recipe. But the constant pressure to create new dishes and to improve existing dishes means that their organized knowledge is constantly in use.

METACOGNITION

Neither the Buckners nor any other experts know everything. They encounter problems they have not seen before and, to solve them, they try analogies with problems that they do know about. In the process, they can make mistakes. But here, too, there are better and worse ways to proceed. In particular, experts are adept at metacognition—the ability to step back to consider how a current problem-solving strategy is performing, and to switch to an alternative strategy when the initial strategy no longer seems promising. Metacognition is an awkward concept—the act of thinking about how one is thinking—but it is how experts avoid dead ends. Depending on the problem, metacognition can require several types of knowledge: a sense of when to give up on a strategy, a knowledge of alternative strategies, the good judgment about the strategy to try next.

Andy Cooper is chief information officer at a firm we will call Recruit.ASP, a firm that specializes in recruiting scientific personnel.[11] By the late 1990s, the firm had built up a large portfolio of products ranging from setting up recruiting booths at job fairs to web-based recruiting to software that enabled large companies to automate parts of their own scientific recruiting. While some of these products had been internally developed, most had come through the acquisition of smaller firms.

The various products had very different sales cycles. A salesperson who sold job-fair booths expected to call between seventy and a hundred potential clients each day to generate sales. If a customer wanted a booth, the sale was typically finalized in that phone call or a subsequent one, generating several thousand dollars for the company. When the call was completed, the salesperson would hand off the information as quickly as possible to others who would actually set up the booth and do the billing, while the salesperson returned to making calls. Salespeople for the automated recruiting software made fewer calls and spent more time designing specific proposals. Their sales cycle involved twenty steps that could take six to twenty months to complete. A software sale could earn the company several hundred thousand to a million dollars.

All Recruit.ASP sales workers use software to identify and contact clients. When the firm acquired a new company, its salesforce continued to use the package it had been using, a situation that began to create problems. Salespeople selling simpler products—such as job-fair booths—used software that focused on contacts. It produced a list of potential customers and automatically dialed their numbers but did nothing else. Once a sale was made, the salesperson wrote the information on a card, which might or might not make its way to all the relevant departments. The lack of a comprehensive data system prevented managers from easily determining how much business had been sold or billed or paid for. Managers also suspected that the firm was missing opportunities for cross-selling—attracting customers of simple products to more complex, higher-profit products.

To solve these problems, Cooper was charged with putting all salesworkers on the same information system that would record the details of each sale and make this information accessible to all departments. He approached the problem by assessing the information needs of each sales group and the relevant operational departments. After some discussion, he and his staff chose the package already being used by the group selling automated recruiting software. It had good record-keeping features and its extensive information requirements were sufficient to satisfy everyone's needs.

The implementation went fairly smoothly and soon all sales groups were using the common package. As time passed, however, Cooper realized that the solution wasn't working. Even though there were no breakdowns and operational departments were happy with the data they were receiving, Cooper, in various ways, began to see that sellers of simpler products disliked the software. As Cooper explored the situation with these salespeople, he realized that his initial understanding of their job had overlooked an important dimension. To make money, they needed to make a great many calls each day. The new system's data-entry requirements slowed them down and left them frustrated.

Once Cooper understood the situation, he altered his approach to the problem. For these salespeople, he designed a new computer interface that required less data entry and reduced the time between calls. The morale of the salespeople improved.

We can visualize this process—attempting a solution, reflecting on how well it works, perhaps selecting an alternative approach—in many problem-solving activities: diagnosing a patient, creating a new dish, writing a report, structuring a financial transaction, planting a garden on shady ground.[12] We can visualize the process in trying to convey a specific meaning to another person (chapter 5). In many such situations, there is no definitive signal that a solution is failing. The individual must make that judgment by processing the information that the situation provides. The processing relies on pattern recognition, where the context is formed by the individual's knowledge and experience. As this description suggests, metacognition—deciding when and how to change problem-solving strategies—is not something computers do well. Computers can complement human metacognition by providing supporting information, but metacognition, so important to expert thinking and complex communication, remains a distinctly human skill.[13]

SUPPORTING EXPERT THINKING

At the level of theory, it is clear how computers shift human work toward expert thinking. At the level of practice, the shift begins with a supply of people who have learned to solve problems that defy rules-based solutions. In chapters 7 and 8 we discuss education and training programs that help develop these skills. But the shift also requires a workplace design that supports the development and exercise of expertise.

Learning Organizations

Sometimes, the "workplace" must be defined broadly. Recall the Xerox service technicians described by Julian Orr. Over time, each technician acquired a great deal of knowledge relevant to repairing complex copying machines, but individual technicians learned different things. As a result, what they knew collectively was much more than what each knew individually. Figuring out how to share this knowledge was critical to making their jobs easier. Their solution was to eat breakfast together regularly and swap war stories. The breakfast conversations became a critical mechanism for developing common expertise. While the breakfast solution worked for technicians who were on the road early every day, sharing expertise more typically requires an organizational design that promotes learning and joint problem solving.

The technicians' accumulation of knowledge was, in economic terms, a public good. Unlike a private good—say, a cup of coffee—each technician could use the knowledge without diminishing the knowledge available for everyone else. But public goods run the risk of free riders—people who want to use the good without making contributions of their own. In the case of the Xerox technicians, free riders were not an issue. Eating breakfast together and telling stories are fun, and a technician who was silent and only took notes would soon lose his place at the table. But if contributing to knowledge involves more work—say, writing up a case for a workplace database—the free rider problem is potentially more serious. Earlier, we discussed the possibility that persons who solve new problems could document their solutions so that others could learn from them. Under what circumstances does documentation of solutions work?

At the outset, the success of documentation hinges on the ability of text and pictures—the standard media—to convey the problem adequately. Given the right audience, text and pictures can convey the meaning of many technical problems. These same media are less good at conveying the meaning of problems involving nuanced human interactions, a subject we discuss in chapter 5. But as we have just argued, documentation's success also depends on organizational design—in particular, incentives.

Organizational theorist Wanda Orlikowski uses the following example to illustrate this challenge.[14] A software engineer works as part of a technical assistance group in a company providing enterprise software to commercial clients. She has just finished solving a difficult problem called in by a customer. The problem arose in a new release of the company's product, and the problem was new to her. She cannot describe the process by which she solved it—there were no rules to follow, and the solution came in a moment of insight. But having solved the problem, she could document the case and give a running start to other representatives when they received similar calls (and there would be similar calls). But documenting the case takes time—time that could be spent answering the calls of other customers.

The question is particularly important in the computerized workplace. If the representative chooses to document the case, a computerized database provides an ideal repository. Information is simultaneously available to multiple representatives. Search can be rapid. Hypertext can cross-reference connected problems that, on the surface, appear unrelated. But none of this means anything unless the representative believes that documentation is worth her time.

The computerized database is another public good. All the representatives would love a well-documented, carefully indexed solution set that they could access. But most would love this database even more if they didn't have to take the time to contribute.

Different organizations have dealt with this public good problem in different ways. In the case of the software engineer, her group was small and shared the same location. When the company introduced computerized documentation, it asked that people attach their names to their solutions, allowing substantial social pressure to operate, just as it had among the Xerox technicians. Strong contributors got recognition. Those tempted to "free ride" knew they would have to face their colleagues.

In larger, more anonymous organizations, incentives can be harder to structure. For example, Orbit Motor Company, like other auto manufacturers, understood the value of having repair technicians document new problems and solutions. Orbit's repair manuals are on frequently updated CD-ROMs that are supplemented by on-line service bulletins. When a new problem is solved, the solution can be sent to dealers quickly, saving large amounts of technicians' time. But Orbit also knew it was dealing with a dispersed group of technicians for whom social incentives to contribute were minimal. As a result, Orbit created financial incentives for technicians to document new problems and send their solutions to company headquarters.

In practice these incentives have proven difficult to administer. To avoid simply handing out money, the company must decide whether each reported problem really exists, whether it is new, and whether the proposed solution works.

Dennis LaGrand experienced Orbit's difficulty in getting the incentives right. One day an Orbit customer brought in a newly purchased SUV with a luxury trim package that included a factory-installed anti-theft alarm. The customer explained that the alarm did not work. None of the standard diagnostic tests revealed the source of the problem, nor did calls to the Orbit Technical Assistance Line. By comparing the wiring in the SUV to the wiring diagram in the manual, Dennis ultimately discovered the problem: two terminals connected by a two-inch piece of wire that, according to the wiring diagram, should not have been there. The wire created a short circuit that kept the alarm from recognizing that the vehicle's doors were locked. When Dennis cut the wire, the alarm functioned as it should.

It took several additional phone calls to discover the source of the problem. All Orbit SUVs with luxury trim had a car alarm installed because this was less expensive than having the assembly line produce some cars with alarms and others without them. If a customer declined to purchase the alarm, the factory used the two-inch piece of wire to short out the alarm. The root problem was confusion over how the vehicle had been ordered—with an alarm or without.

When Dennis documented his solution to the nonfunctioning car alarm, Orbit denied his request for an incentive payment on the grounds that this was a problem in the ordering system rather than a problem in the car. The decision might have been justified on narrow grounds, but the faulty order system had generated a real car problem that had taken Dennis several days to solve. The service manager at Medford Orbit protested the decision, and Dennis got his award. The initial denial and the subsequent delay, however, sent Dennis and his colleagues the message that documenting solutions is not worth the trouble it takes.

In the language of management, both the software assistance group and Orbit were trying to create "learning organizations." Computerized databases can support such organizations if they contain the right knowledge. The problem is creating incentives for employees to contribute what they have learned.[15] As we will see in chapter 8, turning schools into learning organizations is critical to improving American education.

Computers and the Reorganization of Work

The computerized workplace raises a final problem in expert thinking—learning how to reorganize work to take advantage of the relative strengths of computers and people. The theory of reorganization is straightforward: choose an organizational goal; allow computers to carry out rules-based tasks; allow people to concentrate on tasks requiring pattern recognition; be alert for cases in which computers can complement human pattern recognition by providing additional information. Re-engineering, beneath its exaggerated claims, rests on these ideas.

In practice, however, the fit of the theory with the work of a particular organization is often unclear. Even with clear goals, organizations often find themselves at the bleeding edge of technology, trying to understand how computers can be used effectively. The process is made more painful since using computers most effectively may require different human skills. The Cabot Bank example, mentioned in chapter 3, illustrates this point.

Historically, Cabot Bank, like other banks, had organized exceptions processing into narrow jobs in which each clerk specialized in a single exception—verifying signatures or processing overdrafts or stop-payment orders or address changes. This had the advantage of getting the work done even though the turnover rate among workers was high. Little training was needed before newly hired clerks could do their narrow jobs.

The major disadvantage of this organization of work was poor service quality. Some customers who were short on cash would buy time by writing multiple checks to creditors and then issuing multiple stop payment requests. Depending on the timing, each check might trigger an overdraft exception as well as a stop payment exception. If a check were large enough, it would also trigger a signature verification exception. Each of these exceptions would be processed by a different clerk. Each clerk would have only a partial picture of the problem and would have to locate the same paper check in a large box of checks. Often customers ended up being charged (incorrectly) with both a stop payment fee and an overdraft fee. If the customer went to a bank branch to resolve the situation, there was no single person in exceptions processing who would have easy access to all the relevant information. As a result, it took considerable time to clear up overcharges. The poor service quality was very much a function of organizational design. The narrow job definitions provided workers no opportunity to learn how their task related to those of their co-workers.

The importance of organizational design for stimulating or repressing the development of expertise is not a new idea. We remember Adam Smith for explaining how the division of labor—dividing work into narrow tasks—increases short-run efficiency. In his 1776 treatise, *The Wealth of Nations*, Smith also made clear how that same structure stifles learning.

> The man whose whole life is spent in performing a few simple operations, of which the effects are perhaps always the same, or very nearly the same, has no occasion to exert his understanding or to exercise his invention in finding out expedients for removing difficulties which never occur. He naturally loses, therefore, the habit of such exertion, and generally becomes as stupid and ignorant as it is possible for a human creature to become. (vol. 1, p. 178)

Cabot Bank's decision in the 1990s to introduce new technology that created electronic images of checks offered the potential to increase productivity and improve service quality in exceptions processing. The management question was how to reorganize exceptions processing to achieve these goals. The vice president in charge of the unit was both smart and lucky. He was smart because he recognized the importance of employee buy-in. He believed that involving current employees in the redesign would both utilize their knowledge and gain their commitment to the new system. He was lucky because Cabot Bank's purchases of other banks and the high rates of turnover among the clerks allowed him to promise at the outset that reorganization would not result in layoffs. To the contrary, the vice president promised extensive training so that all incumbent clerks, many of whom had never worked with a computer, would have the support needed to learn to do the redesigned jobs. Finally, he promised that mastering the new job would lead to higher pay—a promise that made sense because the training increased the value of the clerks not only to Cabot Bank but also to many financial sector competitors.

Managers held focus groups of exceptions processing clerks, asking them what aspects of their jobs were irritating, and what changes would make the jobs better. The consensus was that work should no longer be divided by exception type but by customer account, so that the same clerk would deal with all exceptions—stop payment requests, overdrafts, and so on—connected to the given account. The clerk could mentally process this information to reconstruct an account's activity. For example, a clerk who saw a stop-payment order could anticipate a possible (incorrect) overdraft exception as well as other stop payment and overdraft exceptions from the same account.

The reorganization would not be cost free. A representative who had processed one type of exception for a number of years would have to learn how to process a variety of exceptions using networked personal computers. But computers made the training investment less risky since imaging technology eliminated time spent looking for paper checks and gave the clerks more time to resolve exceptions.

Because imaging technology was taking time to debug, the department moved to the organization of work by accounts before the image processing was introduced. The result was an immediate gain in productivity. Before the reorganization, 650 workers processed 65,000 exceptions per day. Following the reorganization, but before imaging technology, this same workload was completed by 530 workers.[16]

Even after the reorganization of work, reliance on paper checks continued to pose a bottleneck because clerks spent considerable time searching for specific paper checks. The introduction of the imaging technology solved this problem and permitted additional productivity gains. By the end of 1996, a year after the introduction of the image technology, the number of workers in exceptions processing had fallen to 470.[17] The reorganization of exceptions processing was a major success for Cabot Bank, producing both productivity gains and improved customer service.[18]

CONCLUSION

In this chapter we have described the components of expert thinking: effective pattern matching based on detailed knowledge; and metacognition, the set of skills used by the stumped expert to decide when to give up on one strategy and what to try next. In chapter 5, we unpack the meaning of complex communication.

CHAPTER 5

Complex Communication

IN THE *GUINNESS BOOK OF RECORDS,* THE ENTRY FOR THE shortest correspondence belongs to the French author Victor Hugo and his publisher.[1] After finishing *Les Misérables,* the exhausted writer delivered the manuscript to the publisher and left on vacation. But Hugo worried about the book's reception, and so he wrote his publisher a very short note, which said:

?

The publisher sent back an equally short note that, to Hugo's delight, read

!

Their communication is an information-age dream. Two characters—fourteen bits—posed and then confirmed dreams of wealth and acclaim.[2] But Hugo and his publisher were communicating under ideal conditions. The men had three advantages:

1. Shared understanding: Despite their quirky messages, Hugo and his publisher understood each other immediately. In cognitive

terms, the men shared a context that allowed each man to process ? and ! and reach the same understanding.

2. Mutual trust: Hugo delighted in receiving the ! because he understood the message and because he believed the message was true. He might have trusted the message because he knew the publisher to be an honorable person. Alternatively, he might have reasoned that the publisher had no reason to lie. Whatever his thinking, had Hugo not believed the publisher, communication would have been more difficult.
3. Shared goals: Hugo and his publisher each wanted *Les Misérables* to succeed. Happily, the book's reception was consistent with their common goal, and the communication was quickly concluded. Had the two men been communicating on a different subject—say, how much to spend on advertising and who should pay for it—their communication might have taken multiple rounds with issues of understanding and trust taking center stage.

In daily work, we communicate under less ideal conditions. A mathematics teacher presenting the first calculus lesson cannot assume common understanding in her class—she has to build it. A car salesman showing a Buick Rendezvous to a new customer cannot assume mutual trust—he has to gain it. A manager forming a new project team cannot assume the members share the same goals—she has to negotiate the goals. To borrow a clothing analogy, each communication begins with a set of information that must be custom fitted.

In the fever of the Internet boom, the need for custom fitting was often forgotten. Business plans often assumed that if a web page or email could bring you information, you would interpret the information as its author had intended. In some cases a one-way information flow is enough to do the job. A grocery store can track its inventory using information communicated from bar-code scanners. Martin Luther King's 1963 speech on the steps of the Lincoln Memorial moved much of the nation without benefit of clarifying questions. But in many other cases, communication requires the custom fitting of explaining, listening, persuading, and negotiating. Each of these involves a two-way information exchange. The information is frequently both verbal and nonverbal—what the other person says, but also the expression on her face and the tone of her voice. We process most of this information by pattern recognition and the interaction is guided by metacognition in which we modify our approach as we better understand what the other person is thinking. None of this is easy to program.

The manager who guides and motivates subordinates, the teacher who helps a student to reach an understanding, the salesman who convinces a customer to buy: they have always been regarded as skilled workers. In an economy flooded with new information and new products, the value of their skills increases since communicating complex information is not a task computers do well.

BUILDING UNDERSTANDING

In his message, Hugo reduced a complex vision of success to a single "?" The example is extreme but most messages require a similar distilling of information—selecting key pieces of a complex idea to express in words, sounds, and images.

Receiving a message involves the opposite process: filling in the information that is missing. A skilled communicator knows that a message he receives, like the messages he sends, contains selected information. As a result, it may lead to misunderstanding—it may not accurately convey the sender's idea. The problem is greatest when trying to convey a new idea—an idea for which the recipient may lack the proper context. In a rapidly changing economy, the new idea problem arises frequently.

Roger Perron lays out printed circuit boards for Computerized Circuit Design (CCD), a three-person firm in Salem, New Hampshire. CCD contracts with firms that design circuit boards for a wide range of products including automobiles, home and commercial alarm systems, cell phones, and guided missiles. A consumer electronics firm designs a DVD player with a new on-screen navigation guide. The design requires a new circuit board with multiple layers of components linked across layers. The electronics firm hires CCD to do the layout and Roger gets the job.

The electronics firm gives Roger three sets of information: drawings that show the circuit board's required dimensions and the locations of critical components, specifications for each component, and rough schematics that describe how each component is connected to the others. Using computer-assisted design tools, Roger works with the information to design the circuit board's layout: the number of layers compressed like a very thin sandwich, the electrical paths on each layer, the locations of the components. His end product is a set of digital files containing a blueprint and digitized machine settings that he emails to a fabrication firm that constructs the prototype board.

At first glance, Roger has a solitary job with little need for human interaction. The picture is half right. Roger's end product—the digitized machine settings—can be communicated electronically. Like Hugo and his publisher, Roger and the fabricator share a context—the data protocols for writing machine settings. Because of these protocols, Roger's emailed settings contain all the information the fabricator needs.

Laying out the board itself is more complex. From experience, Roger knows that the three sets of data he received from the electronics firm do not fully describe what the engineer wants, and Roger cannot fill in the gaps by himself. He also knows that engineers are not fluent in circuit board design and that some aspects of the design may be infeasible.

Roger sometimes thinks about working from home since his wife and children are out of the house all day. Gary Abate, CCD's founder and Roger's boss, resists the idea, and it is easy to see why. As Roger does a trial layout, he has running conversations with Gary and with the firm's third layout designer, Ed Dame: "Can you take a look at this?" "Is this what this engineer usually asks for?" "Do you understand this email?" "How would you handle this?" The conversations are needed because the engineer's instructions are typically unfinished. As Roger says, "These engineers are under heavy time pressure, so they send a design over when it is 95 percent done and expect to make last-minute modifications."

For the job to be successful, Roger and the engineer must then arrive at a common understanding that can come only through careful listening and explanation. Often, this requires face-to-face interaction. As Roger and the engineer sit side by side before a computer screen that displays the initial layout, the engineer sees a problem: Roger's tentative layout places two components closer together than the two millimeters required to avoid electrical noise that would degrade performance. The engineer forgot to put this requirement in the instructions. Seeing Roger's tentative layout brought the requirement to mind. Once identified, the problem was easily fixed.

The exchange of information works in both directions. Earlier in the conversation, Roger had broken the news that the circuit board required four layers—not three as the engineer had specified. Roger understood what the engineer wanted: cost is an important consideration, and going from three to four layers would raise the board's production cost from \$28 to \$32. But a three-layer layout would require component connections that can be drawn on a diagram but are impossible to fabricate. This was not what the engineer wanted to hear, but the exchange stayed simple because the engineer knew CCD's reputation for competence. Without that reputation, Roger's redesign could have led to an argument and perhaps the end of the transaction.

These exchanges involve far more than the fourteen bits Hugo exchanged with his publisher, and for good reason. The engineer has brought Roger a new design, including elements Roger has not encountered before. The design was too complex to be fully described in written instructions and diagrams. And because the engineer didn't share Roger's understanding of layout, the design contained some layout elements that were physically infeasible. They needed to talk to work out the design.

As they exchanged substance, Roger and the engineer could have stumbled into emotional territory. Roughly speaking, emotion is a psychological state that arises when events or thoughts touch deeply held goals. Volatility arises when emotions bring on a physical response unmediated by conscious thought—a kind of mental short-circuit. As neuroscientist Joseph LeDoux writes, "Cognition gives us choices." Emotions make us react.[3]

Many communications try to stimulate emotions: the King speech or Michelin tire ads that show tires protecting happy babies in diapers. But emotions also can be an unwanted intrusion. Roger and the engineer each valued their own professional competence—it was part of each man's identity. But they could not reach a feasible design without noting each other's mistakes. The exchange could have become personal—"this is a very basic mistake"—and so quite emotional.

Roger and the engineer did not let this happen. They talked face to face where understanding could be established through both words and nonverbal information: tone of voice, expression, pointing to diagrams. Roger empathized with the cost pressure placed on the engineer, and the engineer assured Roger that the 2-mm. spacing was a detail few people knew. The exchanges involved real teaching—describing the right thing to do and explaining *why* it was the right thing to do. Had the exchange been restricted to written communication or even phone calls, some of this information would have been lost, and misunderstandings, both substantive and emotional, would have been more likely.[4] CCD's willingness to let an engineer visit its office and talk through a design is one of the firm's selling points.

Once the prototype board is fabricated and tested, conversations continue, but the subject changes to the board's problems. As Roger says, "You asked how many times a board works the first time it is fabricated. I would say basically never." A central issue is the responsibility for the failure. If the problem lies in the engineering, the audio firm pays CCD to revise the layout. If the problem is a layout mistake, CCD foots the bill. The problem may lie with the fabricator. The problem is resolved by negotiation, a central feature of much complex communication that we discuss later in this chapter.

There is a coda to this story. Roger's design software is an example of how computerization accelerates a firm's ability to compete through speed and innovation. The software enables him to correct problems quickly without the tedious redrafting of blueprints. The software's output—the instruction files—is sufficient to set up the fabricator's machines without extensive human intervention. All of this reduces the price of creating a new design. And so as the new DVD player reaches store shelves, the audio firm is already designing a replacement with still more features to compete in a crowded marketplace. Soon enough—sooner than would have been the case ten years ago—Roger will be back in conversations with the audio firm's engineers.

TEACHING UNDERSTANDING

While part of Roger Perron's day is spent in conversation, conversations are the heart of Edna Keefe's work at the Murphy Elementary School. In the Writer's Workshop curriculum, students write every day, and teachers engage them in conversations about their writing. The conversations require real skill because simply telling a student like Tamika that the paragraphs in her story lack topic sentences won't result in improvement. Instead, Edna asks Tamika a series of questions aimed at clarifying what Tamika knows about the role of topic sentences. She pays close attention not only to the words Tamika uses in her replies, but also to her tone of voice and to whether her eyes reflect understanding or confusion. The nonverbal information is as important as Tamika's words in helping Edna decide what question to pose next.

The importance of Edna's conversation with Tamika is a critical reason why skilled human teachers are more effective in helping children to learn than even the best of today's computer-based cognitive tutors. Today's computers are not good at interpreting human speech, unless the context is very specific, like speaking a city's name. Tamika's responses, at age 7, are quite unpredictable. Moreover, today's computers cannot process the many nonverbal clues that are critical to Edna's understanding of Tamika's knowledge.

Computer-based cognitive tutors are getting better, especially in domains such as algebra. Experts agree on what constitutes correct answers in algebra and have developed models that infer quite accurately the misconceptions that underlie patterns in students' written work. Computer-based tutorials have also been developed to help students improve their writing. But writing is a more complex domain. Defining good writing is often more controversial than defining correct algebra, and explaining how to improve a sentence can be more difficult than explaining how to correct a mistake in an equation. As a result, computer-based writing tutorials are best seen as important complements to skilled human teachers in helping students to master important skills. We return to issues of teaching and learning in chapters 7 and 8.

GAINING TRUST

A different kind of conversation began in the middle of an on-line purchase. A Lands' End customer—call her Betty—had started to buy sweatpants for her daughter on the LandsEnd.com website and soon had a number of questions. She clicked the Lands' End "*Live*" icon on the website, which put her in contact with a Lands' End customer service representative named Darcia. *New Yorker* staff writer Malcolm Gladwell describes the exchange:[5]

> "What size did I order last year?" Betty asked. "I think I need one size bigger." Darcia looked up the record of Betty's purchase. Last year, she told Betty, she bought the same pants in big-kid's small.
>
> "I am thinking medium or large," Betty said. She couldn't decide.
>
> "The medium is a ten or a twelve, really closer to a twelve," Darcia told her. "I'm thinking if you go to a large, it will throw you up to a sixteen, which is really big."

Betty agreed. She wanted the medium. But she had a question about delivery. It was Thursday morning and she needed the sweatpants by Tuesday. Darcia told her that the order would go out on Friday morning, and with UPS second-day air delivery, she would almost certainly get it by Tuesday. They briefly discussed spending an extra six dollars for the premium next-day service, but Darcia talked Betty out of it. It was only an eighteen-dollar order after all.

In basic economic theory, a consumer makes a purchase knowing exactly what he or she is buying and how it will perform. In the real world, most transactions involve at least some uncertainty, and e-commerce transactions can be particularly risky. Will the seller deliver what you've ordered? Equally important, will what you've ordered be what you want? Will the sweatpants fit? Will the vacuum cleaner really work on both rugs and floors? At some point, the risk becomes large enough to buy from a bricks-and-mortar store instead.

Enter Darcia, the kind of salesperson e-commerce was supposed to eliminate. Darcia uses her extensive knowledge to reduce Betty's perception of risk. The Lands' End website has some advantages over Darcia, notably its ability to display pictures. But the website has left Betty with questions on size and shipping times, and Darcia can answer most of them.

Darcia is Betty's search engine, but with a caveat. Like Hugo reading the publisher's note, Betty must trust Darcia for Darcia's information to be useful. How does Darcia gain that trust?

Darcia began to gain trust using implicit logic, including Lands' End's guarantee to take back a product at any time for any reason.[6] If Betty believed this guarantee, she knew Lands' End would have little interest in selling products it would soon have to take back. Darcia reinforced this argument by her ability to look up Betty's previous orders quickly. The existence of computerized records suggested that Lands' End sees Betty as a long-term customer and so would not mislead her in ways that disrupted the relationship.

But Darcia also communicated with Betty through emotion. Time is money, and Darcia's willingness to listen to Betty's problem implied that she cares about Betty. Similarly, her recommendation against spending the $6.00 for overnight delivery suggested she was putting Betty's interest above Lands' End's profits. There is, finally, Darcia's patience, good humor, and Midwestern accent, which call to mind an image of a person who values fair treatment.

Could a computer take over Darcia's job? To an extent, it already has. Many Lands' End customers purchase items over the web without speaking to an operator. As web-page design improves and information is easier to find, this number will undoubtedly increase. But if the customer decides he or she has unanswered questions, computers now are not much help.

There is some history here. In the 1960s, MIT computer scientist Joseph Weizenbaum created a stir with Eliza, a program that seemed to replicate the advanced thought processes of a psychotherapist. Using a keyboard, a person—the "patient"—would enter a question or statement and Eliza would type out an apparently thoughtful response. But Eliza had no therapeutic intelligence. Rather, Weizenbaum recognized that a good way to fake psychotherapy was to parry every patient response with a seemingly relevant question:

Patient: Why doesn't my mother like my cooking?

Eliza: What is it that you really want to know?[7]

Software that directly replaced Darcia could not play these games; it would need to provide real answers. Given the potential range of customer questions, this would be an enormous undertaking. And for reasons we will see shortly, the software would need to communicate through speech to inspire trust effectively.[8] Speech recognition software does a good job of perceiving words, for example, translating spoken words into text in a word processing document. But processing spoken words into *meaning* raises all the problems of context that we encountered in chapter 2. As a result, software can process words and short phrases in restricted situations (e.g., ordering an airline ticket), but it cannot approach Darcia's ability to process conversational speech.[9]

At the same time, software could indirectly replace Darcia's job by allowing the Lands' End call center to shift to a lower wage country such as India. The move might not be effective. The calls to Lands' End are far more diverse than the calls to schedule GE appliance repair orders (chapter 1), and so it is much harder to script responses. Nonetheless, such a shift is technically possible.

Trust and Identity

Darcia did not take long to build Betty's trust, but Betty's risk was relatively small—an $18.00 pair of sweatpants. The choice of a financial advisor or stockbroker, however, involves much greater risk and so creates a paradox. High risk puts a premium on a stockbroker's ability to build client trust, but the stockbroker has few tools to build that trust. His logical arguments are limited because he and a client both know that what they most care about—the future growth of assets—is inherently uncertain. For this reason, the broker establishes trust primarily through emotion. With the risk so high, the process can be quite complex.

Earlier, we saw how Darcia listened to the details of Betty's sweatpants story. In emotional terms, this is no small thing. Everyone has a story. It is part of what makes us individuals. Taking the time to listen shows empathy, a signal that the listener may be trustworthy. Stockbrokers have a saying for this: "They don't care how much you know; they care how much you care."[10] In a discount brokerage, a broker will listen to a client talk about her golf game and then buy her a subscription to *Golf Digest.* In a higher-end brokerage, the process can be more elaborate including the discovery of a story the client might not know she had.

Nick Murray's *The Excellent Investment Advisor* is a widely read book of advice on how stockbrokers should treat potential clients. Throughout the book, Murray emphasizes the importance of unearthing a customer's true goals:

> Go the extra mile by getting to those places in the heart where people really live. This business isn't simply about making money. It's about making money *as a means to an end*—even if the end is just, "I want to *be* somebody." . . . The excellent investment advisor is always searching for the real human ends—the interests, loves, wants and needs for which the money is a funding medium. And, because she is genuinely interested in really knowing good people, the excellent advisor becomes someone that good people really want to know.[11]

In practice, going this extra mile—something Hugo and his publisher had long since done—involves a complicated exchange of information.

Fred Hartigan and his partner Dan Lundgren are financial advisors who run a six-person unit within a large Chicago brokerage house.[12] Their clients have discretionary investment funds in excess of $1,000,000. "It is," Fred says, "a very visceral business."

Several years ago, Fred was contacted by a potential client named Lisa, who was referred to him by an attorney. Lisa was a public interest lawyer in her thirties who had inherited a substantial estate from her father. Lisa's evaluation of Fred and Dan involved three meetings.

The first meeting was to get acquainted. Fred and Dan asked Lisa about her investments, her history with advisors, what she liked about her current advisors and what she didn't like. The meeting involved non-verbal information as much as words. As Fred put it,

> We look closely at the client's body language. We hear the words, but we look carefully to see whether the words match with their

> legs, their eyes. Are they looking at you or at someone else? Is there humor? Sometimes humor covers fear.
>
> [When the potential customer is married] we always deal with the couple. We see how the couple deals with each other. Is one dominant? Are they supportive of each other? We try to tailor the relationship so that both parties of the couple feel supported. We have to do that to keep the relationship going.

As someone who is good at this business, Fred knew that Lisa was doing the same thing.

> People are looking for the intangibles. They want to know, "Can you be our trusted advisor?" That is what they are searching to answer. They watch for our eyes, our facial expressions, how we treat other people in the office. We do not belittle the competition.

A library of psychological studies supports Fred's description. We believe that while people may lie with their words, their true feelings leak out through their body language.[13] We process the information from a person's facial expression, the direction of her gaze, her posture, and her tone of voice to try to understand what she really thinks. Most of this processing involves pattern recognition and some of it is unconscious.

The importance of body language explains why Fred and Dan needed to meet Lisa face to face. Building Lisa's trust over the telephone would have been harder. Building Lisa's trust through written words alone—for example, through email—would have been very difficult.[14] In building trust, body language and words are complements, not substitutes, and so a detailed twenty-page email is a poor substitute for looking each other in the eye.

Lisa had her money spread across a number of managers, including the broker used by her late father. Her reason for coming to Fred and Dan was her fear that her father's broker was not listening to her and was picking stocks that were not appropriate for her needs.

> For her it was mainly a trust issue. She had changed managers constantly. The managers were not paying attention to detail. No one had integrated her portfolio to see the risk profile of the aggregated stocks or organized the money to minimize taxes. There was no

> theme in her holdings. She was convinced she wasn't getting anyone's full attention.

Fred and Dan explained the services they offered. They could offer modest logical arguments. Their fee was a percentage of assets under management; they had no hidden interest in generating trades or pushing particular products. If Lisa were to hire them, they would treat her assets in a consolidated fashion so they could address issues like overall tax implications and portfolio risk. None of this dealt with Lisa's central question—the return on her assets—but it might differentiate Fred and Dan from competing advisors. Most important, they offered Lisa the promise of attention—that they would explain to Lisa what they were doing and why they were doing it.

The conversation extended over two more meetings. By the second meeting, Fred and Dan had reviewed, with Lisa's permission, her financial records and tax returns and talked to her attorney—what Dan calls the discovery phase. Using the information, they drew up a plan to integrate Lisa's assets and they summarized the plan in a purposely short write-up—two pages of action-oriented bullets. They sent the plan to Lisa with a cover letter explaining it was a "plain vanilla proposal" that would serve as the starting point for their second meeting.

The second meeting was a two-and-a-half-hour conversation in which Fred and Dan explained the plan, talked Lisa through her fears, and described how they would have dealt with the problems she described with her father's broker. While the substance was about financial strategy, the underlying theme was about trust.

> All in all it is somewhat of a performance. Body language and visual language are most important. When they leave the meeting, they probably can't remember more than two or three things we said but they take away a general impression of us—whether they can trust us, deal with us.

If a client signs on (as Lisa eventually did), the process of listening continues:

> We end up being intimately knowledgeable with our clients' families, how they get along with their kids, with their spouse, with

their grandkids. This comes with trust, which depends on communication and attention to detail. It is critical to follow up anything you say with action so that the client knows we are paying attention to details. The client is not looking for perfection. They are looking for the human element—empathy, affinity, that kind of thing. But that only comes with face-to-face communication and follow up.

Could Fred and Dan be replaced by a computer? As in Darcia's case, some of the replacement is already occurring. A growing number of web sites do offer investment advice and execute on-line stock trades. The advantage of these sites is their low cost. Their disadvantage is the elimination of human contact, which limits their ability to build client trust.

In the bubble market of the late 1990s, virtually any advice produced good results and trust was not so important. With the bubble's end, people have become more discerning about the advice they receive. In the past three years, both on-line firms and discount firms (e.g., Charles Schwab) have formed alliances with financial advisors who can talk one-on-one with customers. Despite this change, on-line brokers have failed to hold their market share: In the fourth quarter of 2002, 15 percent of all trades on the New York Stock Exchange and NASDAQ were made on-line, down from 22 percent a year earlier and from 38 percent in early 2000, the height of the trading boom.[15]

NEGOTIATING OUTCOMES

Like Hugo and his publisher, Fred, Dan, and Lisa had the advantage of sharing the same goal—the growth of Lisa's assets.[16] Their extensive verbal and nonverbal communication was required simply to establish that fact. In many other situations, participants have divergent goals and must negotiate a solution. In negotiation, communication involves both building understanding and gaining trust, but it also involves the search for solutions that can satisfy all parties.

John and Patsy Ryder had hired Frank Sylvan's renovation company to gut the colonial-era townhouse they had recently purchased on Boston's fashionable Beacon Hill and transform it into the home of their dreams. The contract was a large one, $750,000. The Ryders had chosen Sylvan because of his reputation for doing high-quality renovations.

While the initial work of removing the original walls and utility systems went smoothly, problems arose as the contractor constructed the new interior. Patsy Ryder wanted many changes from the original design. When Sylvan presented his cost estimates of the change orders, John Ryder argued that the figures were too high. To avoid conflict on such a large contract, Sylvan agreed to lower his prices for the changes as an accommodation to the Ryders. However, as the work neared completion, Sylvan became worried. Beyond demanding continued changes, Patsy Ryder expressed dissatisfaction with many aspects of the completed work. She and her husband refused to pay Sylvan the $150,000 payment due when 90 percent of the work was completed.

Fearful that he would not receive his money, Sylvan sued the Ryders, demanding the balance of the money owed under the contract. The Ryders countersued, alleging deficient and defective work for which they claimed to be entitled to damages. Whatever trust had remained between the Ryders and Frank Sylvan was now gone. The parties were headed for court.

The lawyers for the two parties realized that litigation would be extremely expensive and risky—neither side could be sure what decision a jury would reach. Both advised their clients to try mediation. While initially reluctant to consider a compromise, the Ryders and Sylvan agreed to hire Elliott Mahler, a lawyer recommended by their attorneys, to try to mediate the dispute.[17] Mahler brought to the task more than thirty years of experience in litigating and mediating disputes, considerable knowledge of building construction, and a reputation for honesty, discretion, and creative problem solving.

Mahler began the mediation process by asking each party to prepare a confidential memo describing their position and the outcome they desired. He emphasized that the memo would be for his eyes only. He stipulated that the mediation should take place in the Ryders' home so that he could see the work that was under dispute. He also insisted that the Ryders and Sylvan participate in the mediation along with their lawyers, emphasizing the importance of having the ultimate decision-makers be part of the process.

On the morning in which the mediation took place, the Ryders, Frank Sylvan, and their lawyers met with Mahler in the Ryders' living room. The Ryders' lawyer made an initial presentation, following Mahler's advice that he avoid courtroom histrionics, that he express the Ryders' concerns to Sylvan, and that his comments convey an openness to a negotiated settlement. Following the presentation, Mahler asked a few clarifying questions. Then Sylvan's lawyer made her presentation, following the same ground rules. After the presentation, the parties walked through the house, looking at the work under dispute. Again, Mahler asked clarifying questions.

Mahler asked the two groups of disputants to go to separate rooms, and he then began a series of private meetings—"shuttle diplomacy" as he called it. He assured each group that he would not share the information they provided with the other party unless they authorized him to do so. In return, he asked them to "bare their souls and pocketbooks," and explain to him what they really wanted out of the negotiation.

In the initial meeting with the Ryders and their lawyer, Mahler realized that John and Patsy had different priorities. John wanted a substantial discount on the contract price. Patsy wanted a perfect house. Mahler recognized that the Ryders' internal disagreement complicated his task.

In the initial meeting with Frank Sylvan and his lawyer, Sylvan made clear that he thought Patsy Ryder would never be satisfied. He was also bitter about the Ryders withholding the scheduled payment after he had made numerous changes that Patsy had requested. Sylvan made clear that he wanted to avoid litigation, but he also needed to get his money and doubted that the Ryders would ever pay voluntarily.

In subsequent meetings throughout the day, Mahler built trust by empathizing with each party and by asking questions that revealed how much he knew about residential construction. At the same time, he pointed out to each party the weaknesses in their position—weaknesses that might cause a jury to decide against them. He watched carefully for changes in body language that would signal increased willingness to compromise. By listening carefully to the tone of the Ryders' responses to his questions, he came to believe that, while John hoped to save some money, satisfying Patsy was critical to resolving the dispute.

Patsy Ryder's initial position was that the restoration work was hopelessly flawed. However, in response to Mahler's questions, which were spread out over several sessions, she admitted that most of the renovations were fine. Mahler gently nudged her to compile a list of the specific repairs she demanded and obtained her permission to show the list to Sylvan and his lawyer. This too required diplomacy, because the list was long and some of the repairs she demanded were major. For example, she wanted a wall torn down and a window rebuilt to correct a leak. Sylvan asserted that a minor repair to the window frame would solve the problem. While Sylvan expressed an openness to tackle a reasonable set of repairs, he was not open to letting Patsy Ryder decide if the corrective work was properly done.

After gaining the sense that both parties had come to trust him and recognized his knowledge of construction, Mahler put forward a proposal. The Ryders would put into an escrow account the balance of the funds owed to Sylvan. The contractor would carry out an agreed upon list of repairs. Mahler would judge whether the repairs had been done satisfactorily. Upon their satisfactory completion, he would authorize payment to Sylvan of the funds in escrow.

While both parties agreed with the general proposition, it took several more rounds of meetings to work out the details. For example, John Ryder wanted a 5 percent discount on the total cost. Sylvan wanted to provide none. Mahler finally closed the deal by convincing Sylvan to provide a 2 percent discount as a final statement of good will.

In the end, Elliott Mahler had helped the parties to avoid expensive litigation. As was the case for Fred Hartigan and Dan Lundgren, complex communication lay at the center of Mahler's work. It included determining each party's underlying interest—about which they themselves were not completely clear. Mahler then had to determine the structure of a possible solution and convince each party that the solution was in its best interest. All of this depended on Mahler's ability to establish trust in his character and his knowledge of construction. These are not tasks that computers could easily do.

NEGOTIATION AND MANAGING

Even in Hugo's day, housing renovations were likely sources of uncertainty and mistrust. But the growing complexity of work has made uncertainty and disagreement far more prevalent in the workplace. As a result, negotiation is a far more valuable skill.

Consider the work of managers. Through the 1950s, management communication had relied heavily on the direct order. Most of the work involved front-line workers performing routine tasks (chapter 3). The dominant theory for directing these tasks was Frederick Taylor's scientific management. Under Taylor's system, an expert carefully studies a job, determines the one best way to do it, and then describes in detail the actions that workers should take. Consider Taylor's famous instruction to Schmidt, a laborer who carried pig iron:

> Well, if you are a high-priced man, you will do exactly as this man tells you tomorrow, from morning until night. When he tells you to pick up a pig and walk, you pick it up and you walk, and when he tells you to sit down and rest, you sit down. . . . Now a high-priced man does just what he's told to do, and no back talk. Do you understand that? When this man tells you to walk, you walk; when he tells you to sit down, you sit down, and you don't talk back to him. Now you come on to work to-morrow morning and I'll know before night whether you are really a high-priced man or not.[18]

What Taylor was doing was expressing Schmidt's job in rules. And because such jobs can be described in rules, many have been successfully automated or outsourced abroad. As chapter 3 documents, a growing percentage of jobs in the American economy cannot be described in rules and that is why complex communication is so important in management today.

The recent history of the re-engineering movement illustrates this same point. In chapter 1, we noted the predictions of re-engineering consultants that work redesign, built around information technology, would eliminate large numbers of middle managers. While the predictions were misguided (figure 3.2), they contained a kernel of truth. Computerization does substitute for the part of managers' work that involves gathering and transmitting routine, easily understood messages. But this substitution led to the elimination of only those management jobs that focused on passing along such messages. As John Seely Brown and Paul Duguid write,

> It is perhaps significant that many of the celebrated cases of process reengineering come from a fairly narrow band of operations. Procurement, shipping and receiving, warehousing, fulfillment, and billing are favorites [i.e., processes built around routine information]. These generally account for the most impressive results.[19]

In departments like product development and marketing, communicating and interpreting complex information is much of what management does. Computers can help managers carry out this work by gathering and transmitting raw information at low cost. But the innovative part of the work—the source of value added—requires the interpretation of new and complex information. Skilled managers are good at this. Computers are not.

CONCLUSION

In this chapter, we have described situations in which successful complex communication requires the exchange of vast amounts of verbal and nonverbal information. The information flow is constantly adjusted as the communication evolves unpredictably. For the foreseeable future, computers cannot handle this task. And yet computers are present in almost all the stories. When Roger Perron was not talking to customers, he was working with computer-assisted design tools. As Darcia talked to Betty, she was using a database to check the size of the sweatpants Betty had last ordered, to confirm item availability, and finally to enter Betty's new order. Fred Hartigan and Dan Lundgren kept all their client information in computerized files.

These situations are all examples of complementarity: computers carrying out rules-based parts of jobs so that skilled people can concentrate on the nonroutine parts. We can be quite sure that this combination leads to better performance (higher quality or lower cost) than exclusive reliance on computers to do the work, because these situations all occurred in competitive markets, environments largely devoid of sentimentality. If a website alone could have answered all of Betty's questions and given her necessary reassurance, Lands' End would have been happy to use it. The very existence of a Lands' End *"Live"* icon on its website—the icon that began the phone conversation—signals a need that runs through sales, management, teaching, design and hundreds of other occupations: a need for the capability to interpret subtleties and deliver convincing responses. In an economy flooded with unfamiliar information, communicating complex information effectively is an increasingly important set of human skills.

III

HOW SKILLS ARE TAUGHT

CHAPTER 6

Enabling Skills

WHERE DO READING, WRITING, AND MATHEMATICS FIT INTO a work world filled with computers? In this chapter we explain why they are essential for mastering tasks requiring expert thinking and complex communication.

SERVING CUSTOMERS

In 1975 Mary Simmons worked as a local service representative for AT&T in a small office in the Northeast.[1] Her customer base covered six adjacent towns. She processed customer bill payments and directed technicians to sites needing repair work. She also responded to customer requests for new products and services but that didn't take much time. AT&T offered their customers a choice of two specialty telephones in 1975, the Trimline and the Princess models. It also offered few service options. AT&T, then a national monopoly, offered only one pricing plan in Mary's area. Services such as call waiting and voicemail were unknown.

Mary's job was skilled in the sense that a person walking in off the street could not do it; but her knowledge came as much from on-the-job experience as from formal training. She knew street locations in the six towns she serviced. She had learned which equipment problems were likely to be complex and which technicians worked rapidly. Using this knowledge, Mary could create a schedule of service appointments that kept both customers and service technicians happy.

To do her job, Mary needed to know how to read and how to do arithmetic. She needed to be able to read the notes that customers sometimes wrote to request service and she needed to know how to calculate the amount owed by a customer who stopped service part-way through the billing month. But the demands for verbal and quantitative literacy were modest because things changed only very slowly.

Today Mary is a customer service representative in a large telecommunications company that competes for business in a deregulated telephone industry. She works in a call center staffed by more than 500 representatives who serve residential customers in five states—not six towns.[2]

Mary now takes customer calls in front of a networked personal computer. The questions vary widely. A customer asks Mary how to avoid charges when calls are forwarded from one city to another. Another wants to know whether she can reestablish long-distance service without paying her large overdue bill, because she needs to be able to contact a doctor caring for her extremely ill child. A third wants to know how long it will take to establish service at a new location. A fourth wants to know whether he can save money by switching from local to metropolitan service.

Answers to most of these questions—answers that often vary according to state regulations—exist somewhere in a frequently updated database that Mary accesses from her computer. To locate the answer, Mary has to translate the customer's question into a structured query that the database software can recognize. She needs to judge whether the information provided by the database really answers the customer's question. If so, she needs to explain the answer to her caller. If not, she needs to reframe her query to the database. To put the matter differently, Mary has a job, in part, because the questions and answers are too complex to be programmed in messages like "If you are having trouble with overdue bills, press 8."

Mary also has a job because she is expected to make a "bridge to sales." With every call, she is expected to sell the company's services, including call waiting, call forwarding, caller ID, second phone lines, calling cards, maintenance plans for leased equipment—twenty services in all. The prices of these services change monthly as new specials are introduced. Telephone service itself is offered under multiple pricing plans. The large, changing set of products and prices makes it necessary for Mary to search a second database to help customers determine what options meet their needs. An effective sales pitch, like the answer to a complex customer question, is hard to script, and this helps to keep Mary's job from being computerized.

Mary earns $40,000 per year, $10,000 more than the average earnings of workers with her education level. This is more than most customer service reps earn, a result of the complexity of the services she sells, her talent for this work, and the significant, but waning, power of the union that bargains for her. As with many good jobs, the specific skills Mary needs were taught in a company-provided training program—in Mary's case, a program lasting fifteen weeks. But new products and services keep coming, and so Mary has to keep learning. A customer service representative in a job similar to Mary's summarized the situation nicely: "In this department, I don't think it really matters how much you know but how much you can find out."[3]

LITERACY AND THE PACE OF CHANGE

Changes in Mary Simmons's job began with the deregulation of the telephone industry and the ensuing competitive pressure. Competition, in turn, highlighted two principles:

- Computerization accelerates the pace of job change.
- Rapid job change raises the value of verbal and quantitative literacy.

In response to competitive pressure, Mary's employer sought to lower costs by consolidating small customer-service offices into large call centers. As in other competitive strategies, computers made the consolidation feasible. Large call centers justify their existence by serving customers in multiple states, and this increases both the variety of questions Mary receives and the complexity of the work needed to find the answers. Mary's training has taught her to be good at translating customers' questions into searchable queries. But without computerized databases to complement her skills, she and her coworkers could not answer the wide range of questions they face every day.

Computerization is equally central to the services Mary sells—call waiting, voice mail, call forwarding, caller ID. Each is a computerized service, part of her company's strategy to compete through product variety. But product variety is not a feasible strategy unless sales people can keep track of the products—an impossible task without computerized databases. The same applies to the company's variety of pricing plans. In this way, computerization underlies both the company's services and the databases that make selling the services feasible.

The result is that Mary now has a job in which text-based knowledge proliferates rapidly. This makes constant reading and processing of dense material a necessity, both to acquire new knowledge about the company's products and services and to find the frequently changing answers to customers' questions. It was not always so. Mary did need to be able to read and do arithmetic in her 1975 job, but the requisite literacy levels were lower because the job's information requirements were lower—a consequence of the small service area and the small and slowly changing product menu.

The link between literacy and the pace of change is not a new idea. In 1964 Nobel Prize–winning economist Theodore W. Schultz wrote a small, insightful book, *Transforming Traditional Agriculture,* which explored an apparent puzzle in developing countries. In some agricultural societies, persons who could read and calculate produced larger crops per acre than persons who were illiterate. In other agricultural societies, literacy made little difference in how much one grew per acre.

Schultz solved the puzzle by explaining the importance of the pace of change. Where farming techniques had not changed for generations, the techniques could be passed down orally from generation to generation. In these traditional societies the economic payoff to literacy and math skills was extremely modest.

In other societies, the "Green Revolution" in seeds and fertilizers was changing farming techniques rapidly. Here, reading was important to understand the directions that accompanied the new inputs, directions that were often very different from those for applying traditional inputs. The ability to measure accurately was important as well, since the payoff to the new techniques often depended on the spacing of seeds and the amounts of fertilizers applied at specified times.

HOW COMPUTERIZATION AFFECTS LITERACY DEMANDS

In Schultz's work, reading and mathematics were enabling skills—skills that were necessary but not sufficient for economic success. A farmer who could read still had to be entrepreneurial to risk trying the new techniques.

In today's economy, reading and math are similarly enabling—necessary for economic success but not sufficient. Begin with reading. If all a person can do is to follow written directions, he or she is limited to the kinds of tasks that can be expressed in rules-based logic. An example is making heavily scripted telemarketing calls. While these jobs require the ability to read, they typically pay only $6 to $8 an hour and they are increasingly vulnerable to both outsourcing abroad and computer-generated marketing messages.

At the same time, a person who cannot read is lost in the computerized workplace. Reading well is essential for people to be able to acquire the knowledge needed to excel at expert thinking. A case in point is the transformation from the mechanical carburetor in automobile engines to computer-controlled fuel injection. In the late 1970s, Orbit introduced electronic carburetion control on all V8 engines. The change meant that visible mechanical parts were replaced by opaque computer modules. To help dealers maintain service, Orbit offered mechanics electronics training on a voluntary basis. Mechanics were slow to accept the offer, and the situation deteriorated as untrained mechanics tried to fix cars by "throwing parts at the problem"—replacing one electronic module after another in the hope that something would work. Orbit countered by refusing to reimburse dealers for a warranty repair involving two or more electronic components unless the mechanic was certified in electronics.

This policy forced many mechanics into training, but the first courses had a high failure rate. In many cases the problem lay with mechanics' inability to read well enough to develop from the written text an understanding of how the modules worked.[4]

Writing is another critical dimension of verbal literacy that computerization has made more important. We saw in chapter 4 how a growing number of firms want employees to document their solutions to new problems so they can be disseminated throughout the organization. The growing use of email also increases the importance of writing. Because email is restricted to verbal information, it creates real limits on communication. Yet its very low cost leads to continuing pressure to use it. Using email effectively depends on the ability to write clearly and persuasively.

Similarly, computers have raised the value of math skills. No one is paid a living wage in the United States today for carrying out calculations, but the advent of computers has made more people into consumers of mathematics. A clothing store manager now uses a quantitative model to forecast dress demand. A truck dispatcher uses a mathematical algorithm to design delivery routes. A bakery worker monitors production using digital readouts rather than the smell or feel of the bread. Employees of all kinds are expected to use web-based tools to help manage their retirement plans. Each of these tasks involves some aspect of mathematical literacy. In most cases, a computerized tool does the actual calculation, but using the model without understanding the math leaves one vulnerable to potentially serious misjudgments.

In sum, computers have made verbal and quantitative literacy workplace necessities. The evidence appears in wage analyses that show how the economic payoffs to both skills have increased over the past thirty years.[5] At the same time, we should not think of verbal and quantitative literacy as ends in themselves, but rather as enabling skills for expert thinking and complex communication. The distinction is important because, as teachers frequently point out, "What you test is what you get." As we explain in chapter 8, educational reform in the United States is now focused on defining standards that all students should meet and on using tests to measure whether students meet the standards. The standards for verbal and quantitative literacy developed by most states are quite consistent with the emphases in this chapter and with the recommendations of many blue-ribbon commissions.[6] But only a few states have developed tests that measure students' ability to use reading, writing, and math to develop expertise and to communicate effectively. In some states the measures assessing literacy are more appropriate to the demands of Mary Simmons's 1975 job than to those of her job today. If this is what tests measure, this is what students will learn and not much else.

LOCATING THE DIGITAL DIVIDE

A discussion of enabling skills needs to touch on a final item—the use of a computer itself. Mary Simmons spends her day at a networked computer. She is not alone. More than half of American workers do so, a dramatic increase from the 24 percent of workers who used a computer at work in 1984, when the Census Bureau first asked the question.

The rapid diffusion of computers reflects the ideas of chapters 2 and 3: computers complement workers' skills in good jobs. Over the past fifteen years, computers' growing importance has led to intense discussions of both the need for computer training and the "digital divide"—the proposition that poor children are not receiving the computer skills they need for good jobs.

Is the digital divide real? The answer depends on what we mean by computer skills. In the early days of personal computers, people spoke about information "haves" and "have nots." The "haves" were those who knew how to use a keyboard and mouse and who knew that text on a screen is just as "real" as text on paper. By the mid-1990s, this definition had expanded to include knowing how to use the Internet, and the term had changed to the digital divide.

In the mid-1980s, one could legitimately worry that only some American children were acquiring these skills. In 1984 the Census Bureau reported that only 37 percent of children used a computer in school or at home (or in both places), and they were disproportionately from middle- and upper-income families.

Since that time, parents and schools have both responded to the problem, aided by a dramatic fall in computer prices. Today, 9 in 10 children now use a computer at home, in school, or in both places. While this proportion varies with income, the variation is fairly modest: 79 percent among children with household income below $25,000 and 90 to 98 percent for all children in higher income households.[7]

In terms of basic computer skills, the digital divide has largely been closed. But as we now know, this is just the first step of the solution. The reason Mary Simmons was able to keep her job as its demands changed was because of the things she learned to do with a computer—how to process customer questions in ways that would let her find answers in her database, how to translate database answers so that a customer could understand them, how to give short sales talks about new products and services that some customers find attractive. These were the skills some of Mary's coworkers found difficult to master. A lack of basic computer skills is not what keeps many workers from good jobs.

As recently as ten years ago, the point was not so apparent. In 1993, Princeton University economist Alan Krueger published a paper in *The Quarterly Journal of Economics* documenting that American workers who used computers in their jobs earned about 15 percent more than those who did not. This wage bonus existed even among workers with the same educational attainments and the bonus was larger in 1989 than in 1984, even though the percentage of American workers using computers grew rapidly during this period. The pattern seemed to suggest that basic computer skills were as important in the labor market as verbal and quantitative literacy.

This interpretation troubled many economists. Many firms, including Mary Simmons's employer, had found that a modest amount of training was sufficient to impart basic computer skills to most workers. Consequently, it seemed unlikely that the 15 percent wage premium reflected a payoff to knowledge of how to use a computer. Moreover, one of the detailed findings of the Krueger paper, that workers who used computers for email earned the biggest pay differential over noncomputer users, seemed inconsistent with the interpretation that the wage premium earned by computer-users reflected an economic payoff to skill at using computers. After all, email is perhaps the easiest computer application to use.

The explanation of the puzzle became clear in a paper Stefan Pischke and John DiNardo published in the same journal in 1997. These economists reported that the pattern Krueger found in American data—namely, that people who used computers at work earned more than those who did not—was also present in data on German workers. But they also found approximately the same wage differentials between Germans who used pencils in their work and those who did not. Given that virtually all workers know how to use pencils, it is implausible that the earnings differential reflected a payoff to skill in using pencils. Instead, the explanation is that people who are in jobs that use pencils—or computers—are likely to be particularly good at tasks requiring expert thinking and complex communication, skills not measured in the German survey. Krueger's finding can be explained in the same way. In the late 1980s, the period of Krueger's study, personal computers were diffusing through the workplace and were likely to go first to highly paid workers engaged in expert thinking or complex communication. What Krueger found was not a payoff to basic computer skills but a payoff to the unmeasured skills needed to excel at these tasks.[8]

A 1999 National Research Council report, *Being Fluent with Information Technology*,[9] helps to clarify these unmeasured skills. The NRC report lists a number of information technology *skills* important for Americans today. These include being able to set up a personal computer and use a number of applications, including word processing and spreadsheet programs. When the digital divide is measured by these criteria, it is closing rapidly. Most American students leave school with these skills today and many studies show that training is effective in imparting these skills to adult workers.

However, the NRC volume contains another list of components of fluency with information technology. These *intellectual capabilities* include engaging in sustained reasoning, managing complexity, testing a solution, collaborating, and communicating to other audiences. The capabilities on this list are strikingly similar to the skills and knowledge needed for expert thinking and complex communication—the core skills we define in chapters 4 and 5. These are aspects of fluency with information technology in the sense that people use computers in problem solving and in much complex communication. It is here where the digital divide resides and where the emphasis in education and training needs to be.

Can information technology help in teaching students and adult workers to be better at expert thinking and complex communication? We turn to this question in chapter 7.

CHAPTER 7

Computers and the Teaching of Skills

CAN COMPLEX COMMUNICATION BE LEARNED? WHAT ABOUT expert thinking in a particular domain? Can computers help people to master the necessary skills? We will see in this chapter that some successful American companies believe that the answer to the first two questions is an unqualified yes. The answer to the third question is also yes, with the qualification that great care is needed in figuring out the appropriate roles for computers in skill building.

TEACHING COMPLEX COMMUNICATION AT IBM

Alonzo's Problem

Alonzo, a first-line manager at IBM, heads a six-person software design team. Seven months ago, he recruited Ned, a software engineer with a reputation for creativity and hard work. Ned satisfied on both counts. In seven months, Ned had made two breakthroughs on critical projects, and Alonzo's supervisor had applauded.

But Ned was a difficult person. Team meetings were nightmares because Ned would dismiss others' ideas. Ned ignored regular working hours. He worked much of the weekend at home, and during the week he would disappear from the office for hours. Other team members took note of Ned's office hours and began to leave work without warning.

Alonzo talked to Ned about the problems his behavior was causing, but Ned would have none of it. He pointed to his accomplishments and argued that he was the most productive person on the team. He said he was angry at being criticized and at not receiving the salary increases he deserved.

Now the problem was coming to a head. Early this morning two members of the team had balked when Alonzo assigned them to work with Ned on a new project. Later in the day Ned told Alonzo that he was beginning to look for another job because he felt unappreciated. Clearly the status quo was no longer viable. What could Alonzo have done earlier to head off this problem? What should he do now?

Alonzo and Ned are fictional characters in an IBM teaching case drawn from a real management situation. In a classroom on IBM's Armonk, New York, campus, twenty-four new first-line managers and their instructor, Jim Soltis, were heatedly debating Alonzo's problem. Some brought into the discussion similar interpersonal problems they had faced—problems that lacked rules-based solutions.

Some of the new managers did, in fact, cite rules—IBM policies on attendance and compensation. But what was the place of these policies? Should they drive the solution or should the good manager find a solution and bend the policies to fit it? How does the good manager deal with someone like Ned? Should she try harder to show him what the team could accomplish if he would just settle down? Should the manager spell out the consequences of a prima donna reputation? Were there clues that a good manager would pick up suggesting which approach is most likely to work?[1]

The classroom debate was part of Basic Blue, IBM's three-phase training for its first-line managers. It is a program to teach management skills that, unsurprisingly, makes extensive use of technology. The history of Basic Blue sheds light on the role computers can play in teaching and learning the skills needed for effective communication of complex and emotion-laden information.

New Rules for Managers

Strong management training is part of the IBM tradition—the ability to teach managers how to do things the IBM way. Formerly, in its New Managers School, first-line U.S. managers came to the Armonk campus for a week of polished lectures on IBM practices and policies. Participants found the week stimulating and worthwhile. Their responses reflected the week's content but also its timing. Managers arrived four to six months after their appointment. Their initial experiences had made them well aware of what they did not know. Unfortunately, the timing also meant that they faced their first months of managing with relatively few resources.

During the 1990s changes at IBM put the New Managers School under enormous pressure. Lou Gerstner, the new chairman hired to turn the company around, soon developed an ambitious training agenda. He wanted IBM managers to become more active in coaching—developing and supporting the skills of the people who reported to them. He knew that managing by following rules would not work in a rapidly changing business environment. At the same time he believed that the company's principles and business conduct guidelines were critical to informing managers' judgments and decisions.

Pressure also came from IBM's move into technical consulting services. A Pittsburgh-based IBM project team might be working four days a week at a customer location in Memphis. Managers became responsible for coaching, supervising, and evaluating employees whom they rarely saw in person. When IBM took over information technology functions for companies like AT&T, it inherited hundreds of new managers without IBM experience. IBM's increasingly global nature dictated that new manager training be expanded from 18,000 people working in a few countries to more than 30,000 people operating across the world. All of these changes increased the demands on the training program for new managers.

The Design of Basic Blue

As IBM's management development team faced its new challenge, its options were bounded by two extremes. It could have expanded the Armonk classroom time from the current one week to, say, three weeks. Tight training budgets ruled out this option immediately.

Alternatively, the team could have put all the relevant material into text, stored it on CDs or on web pages, and instructed new managers to read it. We have already seen one objection to this response: the team knew that the skills needed to manage effectively could not be learned by reading text alone. A second objection would have been a lack of accountability. New managers face a stream of technical, personnel, and client problems that require immediate attention. Simply giving these managers access to written information was no guarantee they would read the material, much less understand it.

Basic Blue steered between these approaches. The management development team recognized that much of the material in the New Managers School consisted mainly of rules—IBM's policies governing promotions, leaves, and other aspects of employment. While rules are open to interpretation, their basic substance could be conveyed in text, provided that the text was easily accessible and a new manager was given incentives to read it. Many of the skills needed to manage effectively were too complex to be conveyed in text, but even here the proper text could complement classroom interaction by defining coaching and similar concepts.

The resulting program, introduced in 1999, extends through three phases over a full year, and covers several times as much material as the earlier New Managers School. The program is best understood through a participant's eyes.

Jim Soltis contacted Todd Willis[2] about Basic Blue soon after Todd was appointed manager of a twelve-person group that installed and maintained back-office software for clients. Jim, who had been an experienced IBM manager before becoming a trainer, arranged a conference call with Todd and Todd's supervisor. He described the program and told Todd it would take about two hours a week over six months to complete the program's first phase. Jim explained that the web-based training materials had been written in simple formats that could be downloaded through a telephone connection—no DSL or cable modem was required—so Todd could access the material from a hotel room or from home if it better fit his schedule.

Todd was one of seventy-five new managers who started Basic Blue in January 2000. The cohort was assigned a Lotus Learning Space, a web-based collaborative learning tool that allows cohort members to correspond as they tackle the on-line material. To get new managers' attention, the first two modules, to be completed within thirty days, cover "keep out of jail" topics including business conduct guidelines and sexual harassment. Each module contains one or more Management Quick Views, short summaries of best practice strategies for commonly occurring tasks such as running a meeting, conducting an employee evaluation, and coaching an employee. A typical Quick View contains a description of the basics, answers to frequently asked questions, "Tips and Traps," and hypertext links to sites providing additional information. Each module ends with a brief multiple-choice mastery test to be completed on-line and sent electronically to an IBM site for scoring. The test is "open-book," and the new manager may take it as often as necessary to achieve a passing score. Scores are returned electronically in a few hours.

Several of the modules contain text-based simulations, short cases in which the new manager chooses among alternative responses at several steps of a personal interaction. One simulation explores strategies for coaching a team member who is not performing well in a new position. The simulations contain links to relevant on-line material and provide instant reactions to the selected responses. In terms of learning by doing, the simulations fall well short of group role-playing and discussion; but they do stimulate thinking about applications of IBM policies to issues that managers face frequently.

As part of Phase 1, Todd had to complete on-line questions about his leadership traits and the organizational climate he was trying to create for his work group. Todd's manager, several of his peers, and some of the people Todd supervised (his "direct reports") were also asked to answer similar questions about Todd's management style. All their responses would be examined later in the program.

To be effective, such distance learning requires two-way information flows. The same software that scored Todd's tests kept the management development team informed of his progress. The tracking was crucial. Often, the time Todd had budgeted for on-line work was taken up dealing with clients' questions. Aware of his slow progress, the management development team would prompt Todd and Todd's manager with emails and sometimes with follow-up phone calls, all reminding Todd to get back on schedule.

Todd completed all of the Phase 1 tests—albeit just before the deadline. He had not understood the details of everything he had read; no one supposed that he would. He had learned, however, how to access the Management Quick Views and what topics they covered, and he found himself returning to them for tips when new questions arose.

Todd's reward for completing Phase 1 by the deadline was admission to Phase 2, the week at the IBM Learning Center in Armonk. It was a week spent in excellent accommodations, away from daily pressures, with the chance to explore what it means to manage other people.

During the week, Todd's cohort was divided into three groups of twenty-five new managers. Some, like Todd, managed groups providing technical services to clients. Others managed product development groups or human resource specialists. Some had been managers for only a few months. Others had significant managerial experience with other firms, and had recently joined IBM.

Throughout the week, Todd's group was led by Jim Soltis. Jim began by describing his twenty-year career history as an IBM manager, most recently his responsibility for IBM's corporate account with Johnson & Johnson. He made clear he knew what IBM managers faced. He explained that the week's purpose was to learn from each other and to see how the Phase 1 materials could help in managing interpersonal relationships—with clients, with team members, with peers. He would not lecture. Rather, he would lead the group through a variety of interactive tasks to help them become more aware of their strengths and limitations as managers and to experiment with strategies for improvement. He assured the participants that their performances during the week would not be graded nor would reports be sent to their managers. This was a week to "discuss the undiscussable."

Reallocating Human Effort

There is more to describe about Basic Blue, but it is useful to take a step back to see how computers complemented the face-to-face classroom interactions. In designing Basic Blue, IBM's management development team used web-based technology in five ways:

- to convey text-based training materials, including company policies and tips on managing the IBM way;
- to keep track of new managers' progress in studying these materials;
- to create virtual collaboration forums in which new managers in the same training cohort could discuss training material and tests;
- to provide hypertext links to fully documented company policies providing greater detail than the training course materials; and
- to provide interactive text-based simulations that offered new managers opportunities to apply IBM policies to specific management challenges such as evaluating and coaching direct reports.

Through these applications, the management design team was applying an idea we have seen in other settings: let computers carry out rules-based tasks and shift human work—in this case, the teacher's work in the classroom—to tasks involving requesting, interpreting, and conveying complex information, all of which involve pattern recognition.

Moving delivery of information about IBM policies, practices, and basic management knowledge to the Phase 1 web-based curriculum provided new managers with tools as they were beginning their jobs—not six months later. It also freed up time in the Phase 2 week in Armonk to focus on management skills that could be learned only through human interactions.

Teaching Complex Communication Skills

The week at Armonk began with an exploration of different managerial styles: coercively ordering an employee, leading by setting a pace for a team, democratically eliciting the views of subordinates. Here and elsewhere during the week, Jim Soltis could begin the session knowing the class had already been exposed to these ideas in Phase 1.

As a result, Soltis's opening remarks were minimal, and he focused on group exercises and discussion. In one role-playing exercise, Carol Dorsey, a new IBM manager from Atlanta, demonstrated coercion by demanding that an angry employee who might have brought a gun to work (played by Todd) give her his security badge and leave the building. Carol's performance was compelling in part because she had faced a similar situation as a new manager for another company. The other class members watched in rapt silence as the skit unfolded. Their expressions made it clear they were watching a dress rehearsal of something they thought they could one day face.

Soltis then asked the group to discuss the circumstances under which this kind of coercive management style was appropriate—situations in which safety concerns mandated immediate compliance. He kept his role to a minimum. Lecturing would have left less time for role-playing and discussion—now the main reasons for coming to Armonk. As the day progressed, the group used role-playing and discussion to explore other management styles.

The group would return to management styles later in the week in discussing detailed cases like Alonzo's problem with Ned, cases in which it was not clear which management styles were appropriate. The managers identified with the problems—a rancorous interaction between an IBM project manager and a client, an employee who might have an alcohol problem. Increasingly, the managers began to explore how they could elicit information—verbal and non-verbal—that might provide early warnings of trouble. The managers also began to mention policies they had studied in Phase 1. Soltis would ask how the policies might be of help, guiding discussion while remaining alert for unanticipated responses. The discussion was sometimes heated, in part because the managers were revisiting decisions they had made on their own jobs.

In the middle of the week, Soltis led the new managers through assessments of their own management styles—using information that they, their managers, their colleagues, and their direct reports had provided during Phase 1. Because the group had now spent several days examining management styles, understanding one's own tendencies took on greater importance. Equally important was understanding how others saw you. Todd had seen himself as a pace setter, leading the group by defining clear goals and leading the charge toward these goals. His team members saw little of that and viewed Todd as coaching and affiliative, roles he did not see himself in. Soltis led the participants through exercises that examined how their peers, subordinates, and supervisors saw them and encouraged them to translate this knowledge into ideas for managing more effectively.

From Knowledge to Action

Where the primary focus of Phase 1 was conveying background information, Phase 2 focused on changing behavior. Behavior change rarely occurs without follow-up. For this reason, one of the final activities in the week required Todd and the other new managers to construct Individual Development Plans and Organizational Action Plans. These were detailed descriptions of concrete steps they would take to translate the week's lessons into improvements in their own managing and into enhancements in their teams' skills. The new managers shared their plans with each other, swapping ideas for improving them.

The individual and organizational plans were a natural transition into Phase 3 of Basic Blue. One part of Phase 3 involved another round of online learning, similar to Phase 1. New managers worked to develop their skills in areas like creating strong teams, networking, and making mobile management work. While some of these topics were mandatory, others reflected learning commitments managers had made in their Individual Development Plans.

Additionally, as part of Phase 3, Todd and the other new managers had to schedule meetings with both their supervising manager and their direct reports to discuss their Individual Development Plans and Organizational Action Plans. In the meeting with direct reports, Todd explained his goals for the team and his plans to realize these goals. His meeting with his boss, which took place ninety days after completion of Phase 2, was to review progress toward the IDP and OAP goals. Todd's boss had to sign off on Todd's progress as part of the certification that Todd had completed Basic Blue. Completion is important because it starts the clock toward the next round of IBM management training and to subsequent promotions.

Making Basic Blue Work

Face-to-face debate, discussion, and role-playing are central to Basic Blue. However, computers complement these expensive activities by helping participants to learn rules-based information outside of class. In the process of making this hybrid model work, the IBM design team learned four lessons.

Know the Curriculum and the Audience

The management development team had to understand which parts of the curriculum new managers could learn by reading web-based text and which parts required face-to-face classroom interactions.

Get the Right Mix of Teaching Skills

The content of the classroom curriculum dictated the requirements for teachers. The team had first thought that Basic Blue could use the instructors who had lectured in the New Managers School. It soon learned otherwise: facilitating rich discussions of management issues required different skills than lecturing about company policies. In a Basic Blue classroom, the facilitator needed to understand managing the IBM way—knowledge acquired only through first-hand management experience. The facilitator also needed to know how to guide intense discussions among very different people who worked in a variety of management positions. Instead of searching for experts on particular company policies, the management development team recruited individuals like Jim Soltis who had IBM management experience and were interested in spending two years working in the classroom. It then helped the interested managers to strengthen their facilitation skills.

Get the Technology Right

Basic Blue was designed for new IBM managers all over the world, many of whom access the web with telephone modems rather than high-speed fiber optic cables. Faced with this problem, the Management Development Team could have placed the curriculum on compact disks. The team rejected this approach because it knew frequent curriculum revisions would be required in response to both weaknesses identified by program participants and changes in company policies—the subject of much of the on-line curriculum. The web-based approach made it possible to give all users immediate access to curriculum revisions.

In implementing the web-based approach, the team learned that it was important to keep graphics simple so that download times would be short. It also decided against the use of audio because poor synchronization of audio and video streams would be a major distraction for learners. The team also learned that the technology had to include the ability to track student progress.

Create the Right Incentives

When the management development team launched Basic Blue, it assumed that a good curriculum and the chance to come to Armonk would be enough incentive for new managers to devote two hours each week to completing the learning tasks. It soon learned that job pressures caused many new managers to fall behind. The team adopted a variety of tactics to keep the new managers working at the Phase 1 tasks, including using the tracking system to target emails and telephone calls to Todd and his manager urging Todd to catch up.

Incentives were also required in Phase 3, when knowledge is turned into performance. The Basic Blue curriculum focuses directly on the skills managers need to manage effectively. But even the best training can be ineffective as people, confronted with stress, fall back into familiar habits. The requirement to design an Individual Development Plan and an Organizational Action Plan was intended to focus the new manager's attention on concrete goals and the steps needed to reach them. The required Phase 3 meetings with supervisors and with direct reports made more visible the commitments of Basic Blue participants to translate new learning into new behavior.

The four lessons are interconnected. For example, IBM had great flexibility in deciding how to use classroom time in Basic Blue because it could draw on a wide range of potential instructors. On the other hand, the decision to make Basic Blue available to managers who accessed the

Internet through relatively low-speed telephone modems limited the design of the interactions that were part of Phases 1 and 3.

While the four lessons from Basic Blue are relevant to all uses of computer technology in education and training, their detailed application depends on both a program's learning goals and its audience. To illustrate this, we turn to the story of Cisco Networking Academies.

TEACHING EXPERT THINKING AT CISCO NETWORKING ACADEMIES

George Ward's Problem

In 1993, John Morgridge, then CEO of Cisco Systems, the industry leader in computer networking hardware, hired George Ward to help build Cisco's market in educational institutions. Ward, a consulting engineer and former head of World Wide Networks at Motorola, was well suited to the task. He understood networks and he liked working with educators to design networks that met their schools' needs.

Under Ward, Cisco's sales to schools increased, but increased sales brought a serious problem. Many school districts lacked the expertise to maintain the networks. Nor did they have the funds to contract out network maintenance. In Ward's words, "I'd go in and design [networks] and build them and leave, and they would crash. There was limited support staff, and even more limited training."[3]

Ward responded by developing a forty-hour training program to teach networking skills to school personnel so they could maintain their networks. The program included a PowerPoint presentation and a variety of hands-on activities. For a year he taught the program himself in sites across the country. The program proved so popular that he could not meet the demand. He realized that Cisco needed another strategy to create network expertise in school districts.

In the course of his teaching, Ward had an experience that suggested a new approach. At some sites, schools allowed high school students to sit in on the training. Ward found that the students often grasped the critical skills more quickly than the adults. This led him to wonder whether

Cisco should develop a training program for students that focused on maintaining networks. When Ward took the idea to John Morgridge, the CEO was initially skeptical that high school students could learn the principles that underlie network design, a prerequisite for effective troubleshooting. Nonetheless, Morgridge endorsed Ward's idea and provided corporate funding for the next steps.

Recognizing he knew little about developing a good educational program, Ward recruited Alex Belous, the director of Technology Education for the State of Arizona, to work with him. Belous's career history was very different from Ward's. After graduating from college in 1973, Belous taught first grade and later high school in Cave Creek, a rural community forty miles from Phoenix. In his twelve years at Cave Creek, Belous came to understand the myriad problems that fiscally constrained school districts face in educating students, especially in fields where knowledge changes rapidly.

Belous was a great find for Ward. He understood curriculum development and the types of challenges that high school teachers would face in teaching technological skills to students. He also shared Ward's interest in using technology to improve the quality of education provided to low-income students.

Teaching Expert Thinking

In October 1997 John Morgridge officially introduced the Cisco Networking Academy® program. In that month, sixty-four high schools in seven states were teaching the first semester of the Academy curriculum. Over the next six years the program grew extremely rapidly, not only in high schools, but in community colleges, in community-based organizations, and in a variety of other settings in the United States and in other countries. In the fall of 2003, more than a half million students participated in a sequence of sixteen courses in more than 10,000 Cisco Networking Academies located in all fifty states and in 152 countries.

In scaling up George Ward's forty-hour training program, Alex Belous's team faced two problems that IBM had not faced.[4] While all of the participants in Basic Blue were quite well educated and were highly motivated to succeed, most of the students in the Cisco Networking Academies were adolescents with widely varying cognitive skills and motivation levels. In addition, while IBM could actively recruit instructors like Jim Soltis, the Cisco Networking Academies team had no control over the instructors whom local high schools and community colleges recruited to teach the Cisco networking curriculum. The design team tailored the use of technology to these problems. The result is a curriculum that has served hundreds of thousands of students. Its design illustrates the same lessons learned by the designers of IBM's Basic Blue.

Know the Curriculum and the Students

From the outset, the Academy development team decided that the curriculum would be delivered on-line. This made sense because much of the electronics theory and technical vocabulary needed to do expert thinking in the domain of computer networks is based on rules and well-defined relationships that could be learned, at least initially, by studying a well-designed on-line curriculum. On-line delivery also made it easy to disseminate curricular revisions as network technology evolved.

In designing the on-line curriculum, the group faced three challenges. The first was putting classroom time to the best use. The development team recognized that an understanding of networks only began with on-line text. Students also needed hands-on experience to learn both to apply networking theory to solving practical problems and to become more proficient at metacognition—knowing when to drop an unfruitful problem-solving strategy and what to try next (chapter 4). For this reason, the curriculum design divided classroom time between explanation of the on-line text and a great many hands-on activities that students would tackle in groups.

The group's second challenge was to make the curriculum as accessible as possible without watering it down so much that students would not develop real expertise. To accomplish this, the team hired subject matter specialists and high school teachers to work together in writing and reviewing text, with the goal of maintaining a ninth-grade reading level. The team also adopted a format that allowed instructors to choose their own pace in moving through the material. For example, students at the New Hampshire Technical Institute complete two sequential courses in each academic semester, while some high school students spend the whole academic year on each course.

A third challenge was to provide rapid and informative feedback about students' skill mastery so that they and their teachers could quickly remedy gaps in knowledge that would hamper progress through the sequential curriculum. To deal with this problem, the team hired John Behrens, a testing expert at Arizona State University. Behrens and his colleagues saw that computer technology could play an important role in assessment. An early effort was the development of on-line chapter and end-of-semester tests. These on-line, multiple-choice tests, graded at a central facility, give students almost instantaneous feedback on their performance. The feedback received by a student includes links to those sections of the curriculum a student does not understand. The item-by-item feedback also provides instructors with knowledge of the topics they need to cover more thoroughly.

The assessment group also knew that even well-designed multiple-choice questions have their limits. While the tests could assess students' mastery of networking theory, they were less good at assessing students' skill at building and trouble-shooting computer networks—skill that rests on pattern recognition. To deal with this problem, the assessment team developed hands-on tasks that became part of the end-of-the-semester exams.

Getting the Right Mix of Teaching Skills

Since students would study the on-line curriculum on their own, classroom time could be devoted to helping students understand concepts they found difficult and supporting students' work on the hands-on lab activities. To do this effectively instructors needed to understand the material. They also had to know how to teach it, which meant encouraging students' questions and facilitating informative discussions. Finding people with both sets of skills proved difficult. Many volunteers to teach the Cisco Networking courses were high school teachers or community college instructors with considerable teaching experience, but no knowledge of computer networking. Others were adjunct faculty drawn from industry who understood computer networking, but had no teaching

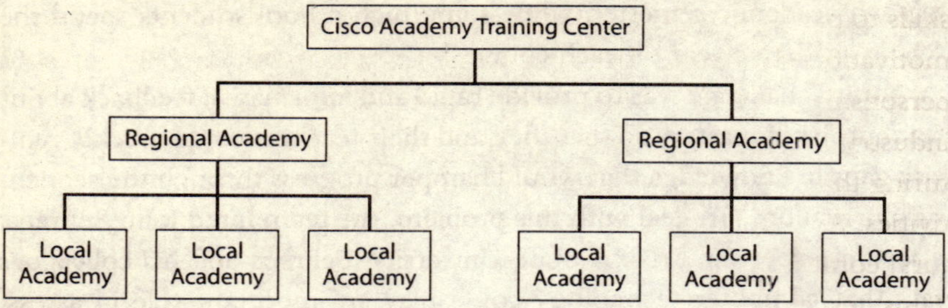

Figure 7.1. Cisco Networking Academies Organizational Structure.

experience. Unless teachers had both technical and teaching skills, the classroom time would be wasted.

To deal with this problem, Ward and Belous developed a highly leveraged "train the trainer" model (illustrated in figure 7.1). The first instructors trained by Ward became the heads of Cisco Academy Training Centers (CATCs). The Cisco Learning Institute pays them to provide training to instructors at regional academies, who in turn provide training to instructors at local academies.

The instructor training program that Ward and Belous designed with the help of professional educators involves eight days of full-time instruction on the first semester's curriculum.

In the regional classroom, instructors focus on teaching the technical material, but they also work to model effective teaching practices. They emphasize the importance of minimizing lecturing and maximizing hands-on involvement. Participants do the same hands-on labs their students will do and they take the same on-line tests and hands-on practical tests to provide feedback on their progress.

To support instructors, the team developed a version of the on-line curriculum that includes detailed suggestions for teaching each class and setting up hands-on labs. Instructors can also access the Cisco Academies Community server website that provides a general information exchange: answers to frequently asked questions, a bulletin board for posting new questions, and teaching materials developed by other instructors.[5]

How well did instructor training work? The consensus on the design team was that it worked quite well in teaching the requisite technical skills to participants who knew how to work with students and had high motivation. Training was less successful in providing teaching skills to persons from technical backgrounds, adjunct instructors who worked in industry. People with this background were often more comfortable lecturing than engaging students in questions and answers or hands-on activities. As one community college student commented, "Some [instructors] come from the field and were not teachers and are not teachers." Thus, teachers' lack of complex communication skills hindered students' mastery of expert thinking skills.

Get the Technology Right

In Basic Blue, program designers and instructors work side-by-side, so on-line communication is most important in dealing with students. In the Networking Academies, instructors are spread out in classrooms throughout the world, creating a second set of communication and support challenges. One response of Belous's design team was to provide on-line resources and chat rooms for instructors. It also provides instructors with two sources of feedback—the automatic recording and reporting of student scores on on-line assessments, and results of course and instructor evaluations that students complete before taking the final exam.

Developing content for students and teachers involved much learning by doing. Initially, Belous's group was pleased with its ability quickly to translate advances in networking into curriculum revisions that would simultaneously reach all users. But the group soon learned that frequent curriculum revisions were a problem. Instructors would prepare their lessons based on one version of the curriculum only to find that students were reading a second version. As a result, the team developed a regular schedule for curriculum revisions that instructors could count on.

While the basic elements of network theory are rule-like and can be learned from text, applying the theory to troubleshooting networks often depends on pattern recognition learned through hands-on experience. This is the reason for the hands-on labs. However, limits on classroom time and equipment often restrict hands-on opportunities. To address this problem, John Behrens and his colleagues have developed web-based tools that permit students to troubleshoot simulated networks on a computer screen. An example is illustrated in figure 7.2.

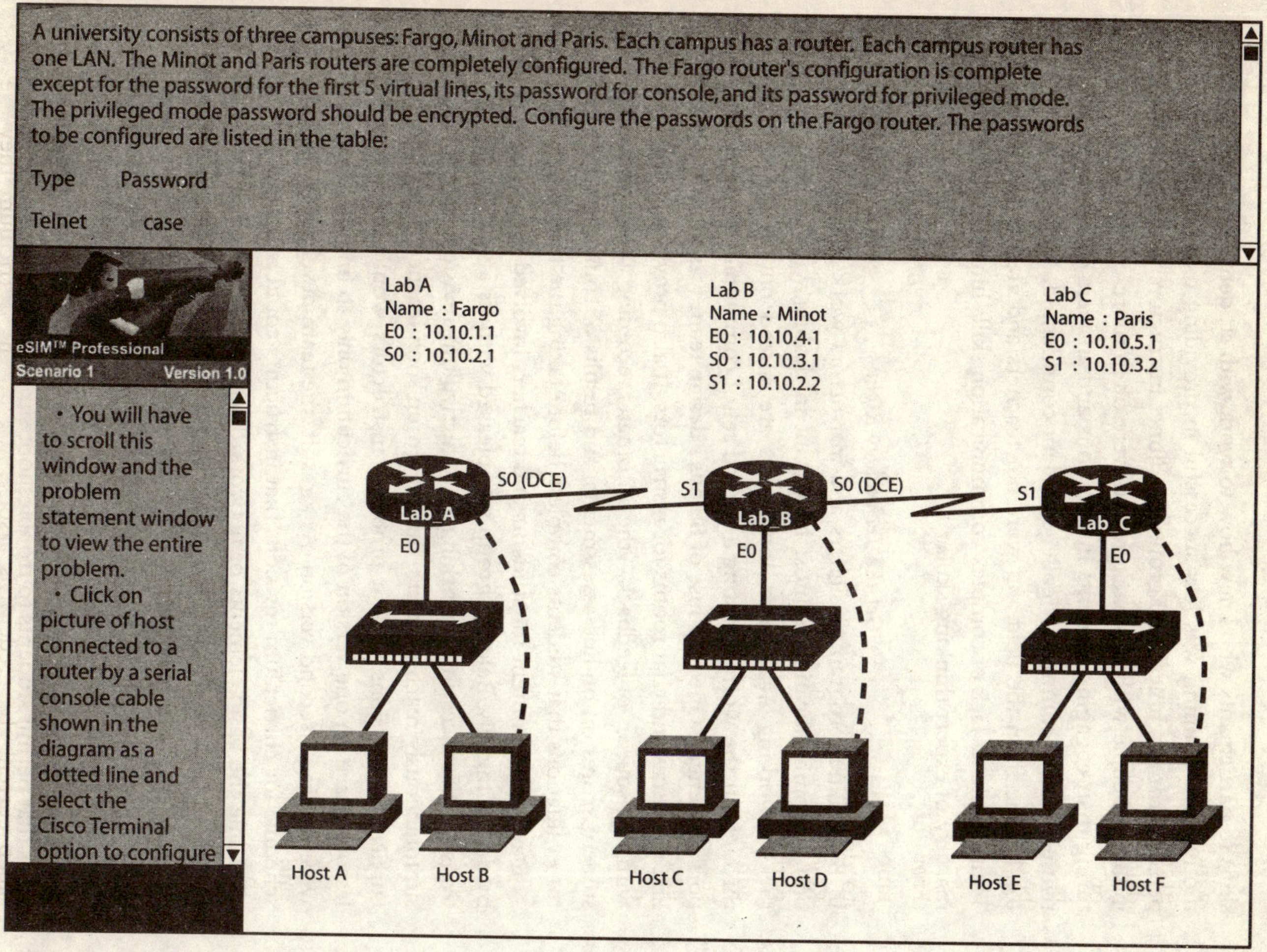

Figure 7.2. Troubleshooting a Computer Network: A Simulation Exercise. Source: Dr. John Behrens, Director of Assessment, Cisco Networking Academies.

The simulation display consists of instructions on the left side of the window, a story problem in the top of the window, and a network diagram on the bottom. When students click on computers in the network diagram, the window changes to appear is if they were working directly on the network device attached to the computer. Students automatically receive scores on their performances that appear in the instructor's grade book along with scoring rules.

Create the Right Incentives

From the outset, the Academy development team recognized the importance of providing students with incentives to do the hard work required to develop expertise in building and maintaining computer networks. Key to getting the incentives right is the alignment of the curriculum with external certification examinations that qualify students for network administrator jobs. For example, students who complete the first four semesters of the networking curriculum should be prepared to pass the Cisco Certified Networking Associate (CCNA) exam administered by the testing firm, Prometrics. As described on the Academy website,

> The CCNA certification (Cisco Certified Network Associate) indicates a foundation in and apprentice knowledge of networking. CCNA certified professionals can install, configure, and operate LAN, WAN, and dial access services for small networks (100 nodes or fewer), including but not limited to use of these protocols: IP, IGRP, Serial, Frame Relay, IP RIP, VLANs, RIP, Ethernet, Access Lists.

Of course, incentives for instructors to develop their pedagogical skills and to keep current on technology are also important. As we have seen, this is a particularly difficult challenge for the Cisco Networking Academy program because the program neither hires the instructors nor pays them. The Academy program uses a three-part strategy for maintaining instructional quality. The first is to provide training and access to help so that instructors have a variety of opportunities to gain the skills they need to teach effectively. The training opportunities help to attract motivated instructors. The program also requires that instructors acquire and keep current the credentials associated with the curriculum they are teaching. A first step is to earn a score of at least 80 on the end-of-semester exam for each course that the instructor will teach. Another is the requirement that within twenty-four months of starting to teach the first four semesters of the networking curriculum, instructors must acquire the CCNA credential and must keep the credential current by retaking the exam every three years.

To monitor teaching quality, the Cisco Networking Academy team relies heavily on the results of the on-line evaluations that students complete before taking their final exams. These evaluations identify instructors whom students feel are ineffective. The team then asks the relevant regional academy to work with the ineffective instructors. How well the remediation works depends on both the skills and commitment of the regional academy staff and on the motivation of the ineffective local academy instructor. Thus, while technology plays a key role in identifying quality problems, complex personal interactions are necessary to remedy them.

WHY DO FIRMS TEACH COMPLEX COMMUNICATION AND EXPERT THINKING SKILLS?

IBM and Cisco are successful corporations operating in extremely competitive environments. Good training is expensive. Since the skills needed to carry out complex communication and expert thinking tasks are increasingly valued in the economy, firms teaching these skills face the possibility that competitors will hire away their trainees, leaving them with no return on their training investments. So why do firms like IBM and Cisco invest in the training programs described in this chapter? Why don't they instead simply hire people with the skills they need? Consider each case in turn.

The economics underlying Cisco's development of the Networking Academy program is quite straightforward. Cisco does not pay Academy instructors nor does it pay for the time of Academy participants—both big expenses for IBM's Basic Blue. Cisco has invested considerable resources in developing and extending the Networking Academies but the program began with a clear economic rationale: without trained personnel, educational institutions would have trouble maintaining computer networks, which, in turn, would jeopardize Cisco's future sales. As the program grew, two other advantages became apparent. One is that graduates' familiarity with Cisco equipment increases the likelihood they will recommend that their employers purchase Cisco equipment. A second is that the phenomenal growth of the program spreads the company's name and creates a great deal of good will.

Basic Blue presents a more subtle set of issues. IBM invests in training its managers to lead "the IBM way" because it sees substantial benefits in having all its managers follow a common set of IBM-specific guidelines. This, however, can be only part of the answer since the expensive part of Basic Blue is the week in Armonk that focuses on improving participants' skills in managing complex personal interactions. These skills are valued not only by IBM, but also by its competitors.

Economic theorists have shown that the answer to this puzzle rests in part on asymmetric information. In the hiring process, it is difficult to identify people who are skilled at complex communication. Scores on pencil-and-paper tests don't provide the needed information, which is why neither IBM nor its competitors can identify those job applicants who are skilled at complex communication. Through the training process and by observing managers' performances over time, IBM learns who its most skilled managers are. This information typically is not available to competitors who seek to hire IBM's best managers.

Another part of the answer concerns self-selection. A high level of motivation is an attribute IBM wants in its managers. However, since motivation is another attribute that employers cannot measure with pencil-and-paper tests, IBM and its competitors cannot reliably assess job applicants' motivation. IBM's reputation for high-quality management training attracts to the firm highly motivated individuals who welcome the challenge of improving their skills by participating in well-designed, rigorous training programs. Thus, because of information asymmetry and self-selection, IBM's strong training programs help the firm to attract and retain skilled managers.[6]

The IBM and Cisco cases illustrate that large, successful companies believe they can teach the skills needed to excel at complex communication and expert thinking tasks. The cases also show that technology is not a substitute for face-to-face classroom interactions in some critical parts of the learning process. If it were, IBM and Cisco, both operating in extremely competitive industries, would have chosen training strategies that avoided expensive face-to-face classroom time.

The cases implicitly demonstrate why the nation cannot rely on for-profit firms as the primary institutions responsible for teaching the enabling skills needed to excel at complex communications and expert thinking tasks. Investing in training makes sense for IBM and Cisco, both very large firms. However, most Americans work for smaller firms that do much less training. In addition, IBM hires only adults who bring with them mastery of the enabling skills described in chapter 6. The Cisco Academy programs operating in high schools and community colleges work hard to teach the skills needed to troubleshoot computer networks to a variety of interested students. However, those lacking mastery of the enabling skills are unlikely to master the curriculum.

For these reasons, America's schools will continue to be the critical institutions responsible for teaching American children the enabling skills needed to develop expertise in tackling complex communications and expert thinking tasks. In the next chapter we explore whether the current wave of educational reforms sweeping the country will increase the ability of American schools to meet this challenge.

CHAPTER 8

Standards-Based Education Reform in the Computer Age

EVERYONE AGREES THAT IMPROVING THE NATION'S SCHOOLS is a critical national priority. People disagree sharply on how to achieve the goal of teaching all students the mathematics, reading, and writing skills that are necessary for expert thinking and complex communication. We begin this chapter by looking at one urban school that has made a success of standards-based reform, the policy approach that almost all states have adopted. We then explain why this reform approach is controversial.

ACHIEVEMENT AT THE MURPHY SCHOOL

Boston's Richard T. Murphy School is a large public elementary school in which four out of five students come from low-income families. One in five students has a significant disability, and one in seven speaks a language other than English at home. To do well in today's economy, these children, like all other children, need the skills to excel at communication and problem solving.

In every classroom at the Murphy the first two hours of every school day are devoted to improving students' literacy skills. One day in Edna Keefe's second-grade class, a Writer's Workshop lesson focused on collecting and organizing information—in this case, about the animals that were the focus of their current writing projects. As the children sat around her, Ms. Keefe wanted to know what questions they were asking. The questions tumbled out: What does it look like? What does it eat? Where does it live? What are some of its enemies? Ms. Keefe asked one student to describe an alligator so that someone who had never seen one would know what it looked like. She asked other children to add to the description. She turned to a discussion of how the children could find information in books to answer their questions, and the importance of taking notes and organizing the information on index cards. In response to a question, one boy explained the importance of "not writing word for word from the books because that would be stealing another person's writing."

The children then worked in pairs to collect and organize information on their animal. Ms. Keefe moved around the room, talking with pairs of students about the evidence they were finding, offering suggestions about organizing the information. After thirty minutes, Ms. Keefe brought the students back together to share what they had found. One child explained that nets were enemies of the whale. Gently, Ms. Keefe asked the child to explain why this was the case. After several other children had described what they had found, Ms. Keefe complimented the class on their good listening skills. She told them that tomorrow's lesson would focus on writing topic sentences and reminded them to take a book to lunch.

Writer's Workshop is going well in Edna Keefe's class. Her twenty-three students are learning to organize information, to explain their reasoning, and to work productively with their classmates—all aspects of expert thinking and complex communication. By itself, her success is not remarkable.

Most schools, even those serving primarily low-income children, have a few teachers who are especially effective in helping children to learn critical skills. Usually, these teachers work in isolation. Much of what they accomplish is dissipated when children move on to teachers who do not build on the children's skills. What makes the Murphy School unusual is that Edna Keefe is part of a coherent school-wide effort to prepare all of the school's 914 children with the skills needed to become expert thinkers and to communicate well. The effort involves four common-sense ideas: set clear goals for student progress, identify the instruction needed at each grade level, measure progress frequently, and focus professional development (teacher training) on improving the delivery of the school's instructional program. Equally important, it involves creating an organization where teachers work with each other to implement these ideas.

Mary Russo, the principal of the Murphy School, sees the state's standards-based reform initiative as critical to her school's success. The state's curriculum frameworks have increased clarity about the goals of instruction. Results on the state's Massachusetts Comprehensive Assessment System—the MCAS—provide valuable data to identify deficiencies in children's skills and to pinpoint topics that need more or better instruction. Boston School Superintendent Thomas Payzant's leadership has also been critical. He has mandated that all schools focus on improving literacy and has provided the resources needed for schools to improve instruction. Mary Russo argues that the teachers in her school do not teach to the MCAS; they teach to the state's standards, and the results are improved MCAS scores.

STANDARDS-BASED EDUCATION REFORM

Reading this story, it is hard to imagine why standards-based educational reforms are controversial. The controversy arises in part because many U.S. schools do not look like the Murphy School. Educational standards vary widely across states and implementation of a state's standards varies widely among school districts. Even within districts with strong leadership, such as Boston, some schools are much more successful than others in teaching students to master the skills needed to excel at complex communication and expert thinking.

How did the Murphy become the school it is? We begin to answer that question by examining the origins of standards-based reform.

Roots

By the mid-1980s, it was clear that an American high school diploma was losing much of its value. As opportunities for women expanded, college-educated women were seeing sharp earnings gains but the earnings of high school–educated women remained stagnant. Between 1979 and 1985, the average real hourly wage of high school–educated men had fallen by 9 percent.[1] Both trends reflected the loss of rules-based jobs—blue-collar and clerical jobs—to computer substitution and outsourcing (see figure 3.2).

Historically, students like those attending the Murphy School had been educated for blue-collar and clerical jobs. In most American schools, the skills needed to excel at problem solving and complex communication tasks were taught only to the minority of students aiming for competitive colleges. The falling value of a high school diploma made it clear that all students needed "college preparation" skills.

Initially many reformers thought that spending more money on schools would, by itself, do the job. Between 1970 and 1990, average real per student expenditures in American public schools rose by 73 percent.[2] Student-teacher ratios fell, and new instructional programs proliferated. Yet test scores did not rise much, and state legislators were losing patience with spending more money and hoping for the best.

In the late 1980s interest grew in standards-based education, under which increased funding would be tied to accountability for improving students' skills. At a 1989 meeting of the nation's governors, President George Bush and Governor Bill Clinton of Arkansas both advocated the idea. Republican and Democratic governors and a coalition of the nation's largest businesses came to embrace the approach as the most promising way to improve American education.

Components

Beneath the state-to-state variation, all standards-based educational reforms include four components:

- *content standards* that specify what students should know and be able to do, and *performance standards* that describe how students should demonstrate their knowledge and skills and what levels of performance constitute meeting the standard;

- *assessments* that measure the extent to which students meet performance standards;
- *instructional materials* and *professional development* that provide teachers with the knowledge, skills, and materials needed to prepare all students to meet the performance standards; and
- *incentives for educators* to do the hard work required to prepare all students to meet the performance standards and *incentives for students* to devote the time and energy needed to meet the performance standards.

Standards-Based Reforms in Massachusetts

The road from these national debates to the Murphy School ran through the Massachusetts State Legislature. Under pressure from the state's supreme court to equalize educational funding, the state legislature passed the Massachusetts Education Reform Act of 1993. The legislation promised increased financial support for public education, and the state backed up this promise over the next decade with more than twelve billion dollars in new education aid to the state's public schools. In exchange, the legislation mandated substantially greater accountability for student performance.[3]

Over the next year a forty-member commission with wide-ranging representation created the "Common Core of Learning," a statement of goals that declared that all Massachusetts students should be able to "read, write, and communicate effectively," and "define, analyze, and solve complex problems."[4] In the following years, committees developed curriculum frameworks that put flesh on the skeleton of learning standards—a contentious process with many fights over priorities and details. By the late 1990s, the basic elements of the curriculum frameworks were in place.

Beyond the curriculum frameworks, the state faced the problem of assessments: how would the state measure students' mastery of the new standards? Spurning the low-cost approach of adopting existing standardized tests offered by commercial publishers, the state paid a contractor to develop exams that would be aligned with the new standards. To encourage the development of communication skills, students would be asked to provide open-ended responses to some questions on both the math and English Language Arts (ELA) exams. For the same reason, the ELA exams would require students to write an essay on a specified topic.

Once the students took the tests, how would the scores be used? As a first step toward accountability the state decided to make the tests publicly available shortly after students completed them each May. This would allow parents and taxpayers to see the questions the Commonwealth's students were being tested on. The state would also provide school districts with reports specifying every student's response to every question that affected a student's score on each part of the MCAS.[5] In theory, school faculties could use the information to identify the skill deficiencies of individual children and weaknesses in instruction. In another step to promote accountability, the distribution of student scores in each school would be made available to the media and would be posted on the Department of Education website, giving each school's performance substantial public visibility.

In a final, controversial decision, the state announced that beginning with the high school class of 2003, students had to achieve passing scores on the tenth-grade MCAS English language arts and mathematics exams in order to receive high school diplomas. (Those students who failed had several opportunities over their junior and senior years to retake the exam.) The decision reflected the belief that the schools' accountability had to be reinforced by incentives for students. It was also an attempt to restore some value to a high school diploma.

Standards-Based Reforms in Boston

The new state accountability system posed enormous challenges for the Boston public schools. Most of the 63,000 students attending the city's public schools were students of color from low-income families who, historically, had scored very poorly on achievement tests. Nor did Boston start off well. Between 1990 and 1995, Boston worked its way through four school superintendents, including two interim heads. The lack of leadership was evident both in low test scores and in the absence of a coherent system-wide plan to improve them.

In 1995 Thomas Payzant became Boston's superintendent of schools. From his decade-long experience as school superintendent in San Diego and as U.S. Assistant Secretary of Education in the Clinton administration, Payzant understood the logic of standards-based reforms. He believed that the only way to prepare Boston's students to master the state's learning standards was to maintain a focus on teaching and learning. His plan, "Focus on Children," emphasized literacy and math instruction. It included choosing curricula aligned with the state's learning standards, sustained professional development to improve the teaching of math and English language arts, and district-wide student assessments to provide more frequent measures of progress than the once-a-year MCAS.

Payzant understood that teaching the new curricula well would require a great many teachers to change how they taught. They would need to ask more probing questions, to develop understanding of students' misconceptions, and to teach students to explain their ideas and to constructively criticize the oral and written presentations of their classmates. To help in this transition, Payzant invested heavily in professional development aimed at improving literacy and math instruction. The district's English and math departments developed workshops that provided opportunities for teachers to see the new curriculum through students' eyes, and to observe exemplary teaching of Writer's Workshop and the new math curricula. The district's central office and its external partner, the Boston Plan for Excellence, provided schools with literacy and math coaches for the teachers, and with money to hire substitutes so that teachers could meet during the school day to learn together how to improve their skills. They piloted a new approach to professional development, called Collaborative Coaching and Learning (CCL), under which groups of teachers worked together with the help of a coach to improve literacy and math instruction. The initial evidence on CCL as a vehicle for improving instruction was sufficiently powerful that in 2002 Payzant mandated that all schools adopt it.

Funding this program required significant new resources. Some came from the new state money. Some came from foundations and the business community. In effect, the message the superintendent conveyed to schools was that they would have more resources and that they would be held accountable for using them to increase students' mastery of the skills laid out in the state's learning standards.

Standards-Based Reforms at the Murphy School

In many respects, the Murphy did not fit the stereotype of a low-income school. Its physical plant was fairly new—built in 1970—and included a large cafeteria and swimming pool. Within the community, the school had a good reputation. The diverse student population got along well, as did the school's teachers, some of whom had taught at the school since it opened. But the Murphy students' scores were low. In 1998, the first year the MCAS was administered, 54 percent of Murphy fourth graders scored at level 1 on a scale of 1 (warning) to 4 (advanced) on the MCAS math exam and 37 percent did so on the English language arts exam. Projecting ahead, these students would be unlikely to score well enough on the MCAS tenth grade exams to be eligible for high school diplomas. The scores could be rationalized. Eighty-three percent of the Murphy School's students were eligible for a free or reduced-price lunch, and the scores of other Boston public schools serving similar students were no better. But in today's economy, the Murphy students were headed for economic disaster.

Mary Russo became principal of the Murphy School on July 1, 1999. Her career included a successful tenure as principal at Boston's Samuel Mason School, and most recently, two years with the Boston Annenberg Challenge, helping Boston Public Schools to implement the system's new curricula. During the summer of 1999 many Murphy parents and teachers dropped by to welcome Mary Russo to the school. They brought a common message: if Mary wanted to succeed at the Murphy School, she should not change anything. Russo knew better. From her work at Samuel Mason, she knew that the Murphy's students could learn the skills to do well on the MCAS. The issue was how to engage the Murphy School faculty in this endeavor.

The state had assumed that detailed MCAS scores would help schools to improve teaching. But few schools had ideas about how to take advantage of the new information. The delivery in late fall of boxes and boxes of paper providing students' item-level scores on tests taken the previous

May provided few schools with a stimulus for change. The Murphy was one of those few schools.

Change began at the first faculty meeting of the 1999–2000 school year, when Mary Russo showed the school's teachers a set of May 1998 MCAS questions that a majority of the school's fourth-graders had answered incorrectly. For many of the school's teachers this was a new experience. Even though the school's fourth grade students had taken the MCAS for two years, many of the teachers had never looked at the exam. Mary Russo asked the teachers to discuss three questions. What do the results tell us about our instructional program? How should we respond as a school faculty? What are the implications for my grade level?

Some teachers reacted defensively to the new principal's questions, arguing that they had worked hard and that the patterns are what you would expect, given the school's students. Others were puzzled, pointing out that they had taught the skills needed to answer the MCAS questions. This faculty meeting marked the start of a process to focus the school on improving math and literacy instruction.

By the end of the school year the school's Instructional Leadership Team had devised a whole school improvement plan that, following Superintendent Payzant's lead, focused on improving literacy and math instruction. One element was a change in the school's schedule so that the first two hours of every school day were focused on literacy, with the next seventy minutes focused on math. A second element was the creation of time slots during the school day in which the teachers at each grade level would meet every week to work together on improving instruction. The schedule changes were important substantively and because they signaled to teachers, students, and parents a new focus for the school.

The Murphy School's math specialist, Jack Flynn, took on the job of exploiting the information in the MCAS scores. Learning to use Excel from one of his grown children, he spent dozens of hours entering detailed student-specific MCAS results onto spreadsheets like that shown in figure 8.1. He then highlighted the columns pertaining to questions that more than half of the Murphy fourth-graders answered incorrectly and the rows pertaining to students who scored at level 1. For example, the

MCAS Analysis Murphy School 2002 (Jack Flynn Math Specialist)																		
Item #	1	2	3	4	5	6	7	8	9	10	11	12	13	14	15	16	17	18
Item Type	MC	MC	MC	MC	MC	MC	MC	MC	MC	OR	SA	SA	OR	MC	MC	MC	OR	MC
ST. 1	1	1	1	1	1	1	1	1	1	2	1	1	4	1	1	1	4	1
St. 2	0	1	0	0	0	0	1	1	1	1	1	1	0	0	0	1	1	1
St. 3 LEP																		
St. 4	1	1	1	0	1	1	0	1	1	3	1	1	3	1	1	1	3	1
St. 5	1	0	1	0	0	1	0	0	1	2	1	1	4	1	1	1	3	1
	1	1	0	1	1	1	1	1	1	2	1	1	2	1	0	1	3	1
St. 7	1	0	0	0	1	1	1	0	0	1	0	1	0	0	0	1	1	1
	1	1	1	1	0	1	0	1	0	3	1	1	2	0	1	1	1	1
alt																		
	1	1	1	1	1	1	0	1	0	3	1	1	3	1	1	1	2	1
	1	0	0	0	0	1	0	1	1	0	0	1	2	0	0	1	3	1
	1	0	1	0	0	0	1	0	1	1	1	1	1	0	0	1	1	1
	0	1	1	0	0	0	0	0	1	0	0	0	2	1	0	0	1	1
	1	1	1	1	1	1	1	1	1	1	1	1	3	1	0	1	0	1
	0	1	0	1	1	0	0	0	0	1	1	0	2	1	0	0	2	1
	1	0	1	0	0	0	1	1	1	1	0	1	2	0	1	1	3	1
alt																		
	1	1	1	1	0	1	0	1	1	1	1	1	1	0	0	1	1	1
	0	1	1	1	0	0	0	1	0	1	1	0	3	1	1	1	2	1
	1	1	0	0	1	1	0	1	1	1	1	1	1	1	0	1	1	1
	0	1	0	0	0	0	1	1	1	0	1	0	1	0	0	0	2	1
	0	0	1	1	1	1	1	1	1	0	1	1	1	1	0	1	2	1
alt																		
	1	0	0	1	0	1	0	0	0	1	1	1	1	0	0	0	1	1
	1	0	0	0	0	1	1	1	0	1	0	1	1	0	0	1	3	1
	1	1	1	1	0	1	0	0	0	2	0	1	0	1	1	1	1	1
alt																		
	1	1	1	0	0	1	0	0	0	1	1	0	2	1	1	0	2	1
lep																		
	1	0	1	0	0	0	0	0	1	2	1	1	2	0	0	1	3	1
	1	1	0	0	0	0	0	0	0	1	1	1	1	1	0	1	3	0
	0	0	0	0	0	0	0	0	1	1	1	1	1	1	0	1	2	1

Figure 8.1. Spreadsheet of Student Responses on the MCAS Grade 4 Math Exam. Source: Murphy Public School, Boston, Massachusetts.

highlighted row in figure 8.1 led teachers to ask who student 2 was, whether there was a common pattern in the questions he answered incorrectly, and what could be done to improve his mastery of the critical skills he lacked. The highlighted columns in figure 8.1 led teachers to ask what the particular questions were and whether they assessed the same

19	20	21	22	23	24	25	26	27	28	29	30	31	32	33	34	35	36	37	38	39
MC	MC	MC	MC	MC	MC	MC	MC	OR	SA	SA	SA	OR	MC	MC	MC	MC	MC	MC	MC	MC
1	1	1	1	1	1	1	1	3	1	1	1	4	1	1	1	1	1	1	1	1
0	0	0	0	0	0	0	0	0	0	0	0	1	0	0	0	0	0	1	0	1
0	1	1	1	1	1	0	0	4	0	1	1	4	1	1	1	1	1	1	1	1
1	1	1	1	1	0	1	0	3	0	0	1	4	0	1	1	1	1	1	0	1
0	1	1	1	1	1	1	0	3	0	1	1	4	1	1	1	1	1	1	0	1
0	0	0	1	1	1	1	0	2	0	1	1	4	0	0	0	0	0	1	0	0
0	0	1	1	0	0	1	1	1	1	0	1	0	1	0	0	0	1	1	0	0
1	1	0	0	1	1	1	1	3	0	0	0	4	1	1	1	1	1	1	1	0
1	1	0	1	0	0	0	1	0	0	0	1	4	0	1	1	0	0	1	1	1
0	0	0	1	1	0	0	1	1	1	1	1	1	1	0	0	1	0	1	0	0
0	0	1	1	1	0	0	0	1	0	0	1	2	1	0	0	0	0	0	1	1
0	0	1	1	1	0	0	0	1	0	1	1	3	1	0	1	1	1	1	0	1
0	0	1	1	1	0	1	0	2	0	0	0	3	0	1	1	1	0	1	0	0
1	1	1	1	1	1	1	0	0	0	0	1	2	1	1	0	1	1	1	0	1
1	1	1	1	1	1	0	1	1	0	1	1	3	1	1	0	1	0	0	1	1
0	0	0	1	1	0	1	0	4	0	1	1	3	0	1	1	1	0	1	0	0
0	1	1	1	1	1	1	1	2	0	0	0	4	1	1	1	1	0	0	0	1
1	1	1	1	1	1	0	0	2	0	1	1	2	0	1	1	1	1	1	1	0
1	0	0	0	1	1	0	0	1	1	1	1	1	0	1	0	0	0	0	0	0
0	0	1	1	1	0	1	0	4	0	0	0	4	0	1	1	1	1	1	0	1
0	1	1	1	0	1	0	1	1	0	1	1	3	1	1	1	0	0	0	1	1
1	1	1	0	0	1	1	1	0	0	0	1	3	1	1	1	1	1	1	1	1
0	1	0	1	0	1	1	0	3	1	1	1	4	1	1	0	1	0	0	1	1
1	1	1	1	0	1	1	1	4	1	0	1	4	0	1	1	0	0	1	1	1
0	0	0	1	0	0	1	1	1	0	1	1	4	0	1	1	0	1	1	1	1
1	1	1	1	0	1	0	1	1	0	0	1	3	1	0	1	0	0	1	0	1

skills. The faculty learned, for example, that most fourth-graders answered incorrectly those math questions that required changing a decimal to a fraction. Examination of the curriculum revealed that the fourth-grade teachers had taught this skill in late May, after the children had taken the MCAS. This led them to develop mini-lessons on key topics, which they inserted into the curriculum early in the school year.

While Mary Russo and the Murphy teachers found that much could be learned from the MCAS results, the time lag between administration of the test in May and receipt of the results in late fall created a problem. The school needed more timely information on students' skills and on the effectiveness of instruction. Implementing the district-wide assessments mandated by the central office provided this information. At the Murphy each grade-level team chose a question that students would write about in their fall, winter, and spring writing assessments. The faculty chose a scoring metric that rated each essay in two dimensions: topic development and use of writing conventions—the same dimensions used in scoring the essays that students wrote for the MCAS. The teachers graded the students' essays in their grade-level team meetings, and Jack Flynn recorded the grades on a spreadsheet. The changes in scores between the fall and winter essays enabled teachers to assess how well their teaching had taken root and which students needed special help. The teachers used student scores on the mid-year district-wide math exams in a similar way.

To be sure that students did not slip through the cracks, Murphy teachers developed an Individual Success Plan (ISP) for every child who scored a "1" on either the MCAS ELA or math exam. Using information from students' performances on the formative assessments as well as on the MCAS exams, the plan listed the skills that students needed to develop.

The school took several steps to assure that students with ISPs received the help they needed to improve their performance. One was the development of an after-school program in which the first seventy-five minutes were devoted to homework and extra help. Jonna Casey, a teacher with a background in business who had moved to the Murphy School with Mary Russo, played a key role. She wrote grant proposals that raised money to supplement the modest fees Murphy parents could pay for after-school instruction. She recruited Murphy teachers to teach in the program. She and Mary Russo worked with the after-school teachers to be sure that every activity, from puppetry to music to chess, had a lesson plan that tied each element of the curriculum to one or more of the state learning standards. The school also developed a summer school program to keep children learning and a voluntary Saturday program that focused on MCAS preparation.

None of the activities at the Murphy School is unique. What is rare

are the coordination of all of the school's activities around learning standards, the focus on continual improvement, and the consistent measurement of students' progress toward meeting those standards. Also relatively uncommon is the creation of a culture in which all adults are expected to contribute to the development of children's literacy and math skills. At the Murphy all administrators participated in learning to teach the new math and English language arts curriculum, as did all teachers, including bilingual education, special education, music, art, and physical education teachers.

Students' skill in mastering the new standards-based curriculum did not come quickly. It took time for teachers to learn to teach the new curriculum and for students to learn what was expected of them. But the consistent focus on standards-based skills is taking root. On the Monday after the Columbia space shuttle exploded in the winter of 2003, Jane Corr's third-grade students were writing about the disaster. As the start of sharing time approached, Jane reminded the children to edit their writing in preparation for reading their stories. Raymond was the first student who volunteered to read his essay. In response to Jane's request for feedback, one student commented that Raymond's story had good details. Another remarked that he liked Raymond's summary sentence. Yet another commented that Raymond's topic sentence was great because it provided all the "W information" (what, where, and when), and that she would give it a grade of 4 (on the MCAS rating scale of 1 to 4).

The progress of the Murphy School is evident in its students' MCAS scores. Between 1998 and 2002, the percentage of Murphy fourth graders that scored on level 1 (warning) fell from 54 to 15 on the math exam and from 37 to 11 on the ELA exam. This is no small accomplishment because the MCAS assesses both students' problem-solving skills and aspects of their communication skills.

As this story makes clear, the Murphy's success rests on a combination of factors:

- MCAS ELA and math exams that are well aligned with high quality-learning standards,
- good curriculum that translates the MCAS goals into classroom lessons,
- extensive professional development focused on helping teachers learn together to teach the new curriculum effectively,

- creative use of student assessment results to identify students who need extra help and topics that need improved instruction,
- good teachers,
- a daily schedule that permits teachers to meet frequently to coordinate and refine what they were doing,
- the money necessary to implement these plans,
- a principal who provides the leadership necessary to keep the effort on track.

Computers can help with some of these factors—the analysis of test scores, the dissemination of new curriculum, software to reinforce some student skills. But most items on the list require sustained human effort. And if a school is to achieve real gains, all factors on the list are required. Even good teachers, while obviously important, can't do much in isolation. With few exceptions, the Murphy School teachers on staff in 1998 (when MCAS scores were low) and in 2002 (when MCAS scores were sharply higher) were the same people.

This story, moreover, goes beyond one school. While progress at the Murphy has been exceptional, schools across Massachusetts have been making progress. The National Assessment of Educational Progress (NAEP), a set of skill assessments administered to a national sample of students by the U.S. Department of Education, is often called "the Nation's Report Card." On the 2002 NAEP writing assessment, 42 percent of Massachusetts eighth graders scored at or above "proficient" in writing, a figure second only to Connecticut, and an increase of 11 percentage points over the 1998 figure. Similarly, Connecticut, Kentucky, Maryland, North Carolina, and Texas, states that have been working at standards-based reform for more than a decade, have seen the achievement of low-income students and students of color rise on the NAEP as well as on state-mandated assessments.[6]

Given this evidence it is not surprising that people from many perspectives support standards-based educational reforms. For example, the civil rights lawyer William Taylor writes,

> Today, new forms of accountability and assessment are the best tools we have to ensure quality education for all children. When

> schools and districts are held accountable for the achievement of all students, the means are at hand to force them to improve the quality of schooling provided for previously neglected students. Standards and accountability expose the sham that passes for education in many heavily minority schools and provide measurements and pressure to prod schools to target resources where they are needed most.[7]

Taylor is describing standards-based reforms when they go well. But as the Murphy School's list shows, there are many opportunities for things to go wrong, and this is why standards-based reforms are controversial.

SOURCES OF CONTROVERSY

Starting from the top, a state can develop vague academic standards that do not provide educators with clear guidance on the knowledge and skills students should master. Alternatively, a state can write good standards but then undercut them by adopting tests that do not accurately measure students' mastery of the standards. For example, standardized multiple-choice tests may measure students' mastery of grammar, but they do not assess whether students can write a coherent essay. Reliance on such tests creates incentives for teachers to spend time drilling students on grammar and little time helping students to learn to write well.

Financial incentives can also backfire in accountability systems. A study of North Carolina's incentive system shows that the criteria for a financial reward are much harder to meet for teachers working in schools that serve large percentages of disadvantaged children. The unintended result is that teachers and administrators are discouraged from working in these schools.[8]

Education Week, a widely respected newspaper that rates state standards and accountability systems gives the Massachusetts system a grade of A−. However, it rates those in four other states as F and those in another seven states as D.[9] The many low grades help to explain why standards-based educational reforms have many critics.

The problems can continue at school districts where resources are not focused on improving instruction either because money is misallocated or money isn't there in the first place. The needed leadership can be equally scarce. More than half of urban school district superintendents stay in their jobs fewer than three years—far too short a time to organize and implement a coherent strategy for improving the performance of all schools.

Critics cite all of these problems in arguing that standards-based reforms are a step backwards—a series of activities that actually divert schools from improving education. Even proponents concede the critics' most damaging piece of evidence: standards-based progress is confined almost entirely to elementary schools. High schools, particularly in urban school districts, have not shown much progress, and making high schools work for most students—not just those preparing for competitive colleges—remains the most pressing problem facing American K–12 education.

Despite progress in elementary schools, Massachusetts is not immune to this judgment. More than 4,000 Massachusetts high school students in the class of 2003 did not obtain diplomas because they did not pass the MCAS exams, even after five tries spread across two years.[10] In Boston the percentage of the Class of 2003 passing the MCAS increased from 40 percent on the first test administration (when the students were in the tenth grade) to 78 percent on the fifth try. While this is clearly progress, critics point to the 22 percent of Boston high school students who were denied diplomas. They argue that standards-based reforms unfairly penalize these students, who are disproportionately students of color attending urban schools, because the students did not receive the consistently high-quality instruction needed to pass the mandatory exit exams.

THE FUTURE OF STANDARDS-BASED EDUCATIONAL REFORMS

The problems cited by the critics are real but there is reasonable hope for improvement. No state has much more than a decade's experience with educational standards—the majority of states have far less. As evidence comes in and problems surface, many states are responding. Some have increased the clarity of their standards. Some have improved their assessments. Some are investing more heavily in improving teachers' skills. Some are revising incentives for students and educators.

Districts are also responding. In Boston, Superintendent Payzant has designated improving schools like the Murphy as Effective Practice Schools. The Boston Plan for Excellence is working with these schools to clarify the conditions necessary for success and to help other Boston schools achieve these conditions. Payzant has replaced many principals who have not been successful in implementing standards-based reforms and has developed a Leadership Academy to develop the skills of aspiring principals.

It is still too early to know whether standards-based reforms will improve the effectiveness of American schools in providing students with the skills needed to excel at complex communication and expert thinking in their field of interest. Much will depend on the responses of federal and state governments and local school districts to the problems we have just described.

Much will also depend on how the U.S. Department of Education interprets the provisions of the No Child Left Behind Act of 2001 (NCLB) and how the law is revised over time. This federal law requires that states test annually the reading and math skills of all public school students in grades three through eight. It also specifies that all schools are expected to make annual yearly progress toward ensuring that all groups of students reach proficiency within twelve years. School districts and schools that fail to make adequate yearly progress will over time be subject to "improvement, corrective action, and restructuring."[11] A potential strength of NCLB is the attention it draws to the academic skills of children of color, children from low-income families, students whose first language is not English, and students with disabilities—groups that have historically not been well served by American schools. One potential weakness is that the NCLB requirements of extensive testing and the need to show annual progress create pressures on states to adopt relatively undemanding off-the-shelf standardized tests that can be scored at relatively low cost. Another is the implicit incentive for schools to avoid enrolling students in the middle of the school year since these students are likely to score poorly on the state-mandated exams. It remains to be seen how states and local districts will respond to the provisions of NCLB and how the law will be amended over time.

Finally, the future of standards-based reforms will depend on the number of academic subjects that are tested. As job market skill requirements continue to rise, it may sound logical that mastery of all academic subjects should be tested. In fact, the opposite is true. Several reasons suggest caution in extending high-stakes pencil-and-paper exams beyond mathematics, reading and writing—the enabling skills described in chapter 6.

Since fields such as social studies are so vast, state-mandated tests of students' knowledge of these fields are likely to emphasize the recall of facts—such as the date of Drake's battle with the Spanish Armada—rather than students' understanding of complex relationships—such as why the battle marked an important turning point in European history. Tests that push instruction toward broad coverage rather than helping students to develop in-depth understanding of interrelationships will not help students to acquire the mindset and habits that characterize expert thinking (see chapter 4).

Second, requirements that high school students pass standardized examinations in fields such as social studies and science in order to acquire a high school diploma are likely to push instruction in high schools toward preparation for these tests. Given the failure of American high schools to develop the skills of a great many students, it is important to encourage innovation rather than to create incentives to focus instruction on test preparation in these subjects.

Finally, our society relies on its education system not only to prepare young people to earn a living, but also to teach them the values, knowledge, and skills to be contributing citizens in a democracy. Standards-based educational reforms can further this dual mission if they increase the likelihood that all students leave school with mastery of the skills needed for expert thinking and complex communication. However, students leaving the nation's schools also need to appreciate how new technologies pose a variety of threats to our democracy, including nuclear holocaust and restrictions on privacy. They also need to appreciate the importance of the Constitution and the Bill of Rights and the Civil War in shaping our democracy. It makes sense that understanding these issues and concepts should be a condition for high school graduation. However, standardized pencil-and-paper tests are not the appropriate instruments. We return to these issues in the next chapter.

CHAPTER 9

The Next Ten Years

IN 1960, HERBERT SIMON TOOK THE RISK OF PREDICTING HOW computers would change the mix of occupations by 1985. We conclude this book by taking a similar risk, speculating on how computers will change the job market in the years ahead.

We will not look as far into the future as Simon did—ten years will be sufficient for our purpose—but we will expand on Simon by considering a broader set of consequences. Simon focused on how computers would change the corporation's mix of occupations. From society's perspective, that change is the first step in a longer process. Out in the job market, the mix of occupations can change faster than workers can change their skills—a differential that computers have enlarged. Big wage changes are the result, as demand for some workers increases while demand for other workers plummets. Big wage changes, in turn, spur individual responses—seeking new training, going onto the disability roles.[1] Big wage changes can also motivate political responses—changes in the tax laws, programs to improve education, limits on imports. We cannot pretend to predict this entire chain of events, but we will sketch some possibilities.

MARY SIMMONS'S JOB

A starting point is the job of Mary Simmons, the telecommunications customer service representative (chapter 6). When Mary began her job in 1975, her work consisted primarily of explaining the company's policies, services, and products to customers in nearby towns. She kept most of the information she used in her head. Today, Mary explains her company's policies and products to customers, relying on a computerized database for access to the information she needs. The database's large capacity complements Mary's communication and problem-solving skills, enabling her to do work that formerly required several people—addressing hundreds of questions each day from customers in several states about a large variety of products and service plans.

Computers have also changed Mary's job in another way. Her employer now uses technology to monitor most aspects of Mary's work: how many calls she answers per hour, the length of each call, the content of selected calls, and the number of minutes Mary takes for bathroom breaks and to catch up on paper work. While technology creates the possibility of monitoring, the actual use of the monitoring reflects Mary's bargaining position. Few employees willingly accept such monitoring, but Mary and her fellow operators, despite their union membership, are not in a sufficiently strong position to prevent monitoring while earning their present salaries.

With or without monitoring, it is unlikely that Mary Simmons's job will exist many years longer. To be sure, possibilities for total computer substitution are modest. Many of the answers Mary gives are ultimately rules-based responses, but Mary's interaction with customers is, in computer terms, very complex.[2] When a customer calls, Mary must first extract the words from her caller's conversational speech, dealing with "umms," sentence fragments, ellipses, accents, and other irregularities. She must clarify the caller's problem and translate it into a question that her computerized database can answer. Then she needs to converse interactively (and tactfully) to be sure the customer understands her answer as well as any sales message she wants to deliver.

A little of this interaction is within a computer's reach. Her employer is experimenting with a computerized conversational interface that may be able to provide answers to routine questions. But Mary's job requires conversation over such a broad range of topics that her job will require the flexibility of human information-processing for the foreseeable future.

It is likely, however, that the human will not be sitting in the United States. Other countries—notably India—are making big strides in developing call center jobs like Mary's. Operators are given typical American names and are trained to speak with regional American accents. Modern telecommunications technology gives the conversation the clarity of a local call. Drop-down menus on an operator's terminal contain glossaries of everyday speech so that an operator selling professional basketball tickets will not have to ask the caller to explain what he means by "Shaquille." Since an operator in Bangalore makes less than a quarter of Mary's salary, it is easy to imagine Mary's job moving overseas before very long.[3]

WHERE JOBS WILL BE LOST AND GAINED

In earlier chapters, we saw how computer substitution had its greatest initial impact on blue-collar and clerical jobs—rules-based jobs (e.g., see figure 3.2). The story of Mary Simmons's job illustrates our prediction that this impact will expand upward in the wage distribution into jobs that involve some pattern recognition but still have a large rules-based component. Think about income tax preparation. The tax system is based on rules—rules that are built into software like *TaxCut* and *TurboTax*. While preparation of complex tax returns requires expert human judgment, many other tax returns do not, and so it is not surprising that the preparation of routine income tax returns is beginning to move offshore.[4]

In some instances, this expanded substitution will reach into high-wage jobs. A highly publicized case has been the shift of programming jobs to India and China. We can think of this shift as stemming from the combination of three factors. One, at least for the moment, is the low wages of Indian and Chinese programmers.[5] A second is the way that software code written abroad can be transported instantaneously to U.S. customers. The third factor is the nature of the knowledge required for programming. Creating a *Fritos* advertising campaign requires extensive tacit knowledge of the U.S. market. Debugging software modules for an Oracle database requires knowing a self-contained set of programming rules that is available to students everywhere.

While the movement offshore of programming jobs illustrates that even some quite skilled jobs are susceptible to outsourcing, we see these as exceptions. Our view is that the greatest impacts of computer substitution (including outsourcing) will be on jobs like call-center customer service reps and blue-collar manufacturing jobs—jobs in the lower middle of the wage distribution now paying $20–$35,000 a year.

Thus, our Simon-esque prediction is that the major consequence of computerization will not be mass unemployment, but a continued decline in the demand for moderately skilled and less skilled labor. Job opportunities will grow, but job growth will be greatest in higher skilled occupations in which computers complement expert thinking and complex communication to produce new products and services. At the same time, more moderate expansion will occur in low-end, low-wage service sector jobs.

This declining demand for less skilled labor was implicit in Simon's 1960 predictions and some years later was given a modern face by economist Gary Burtless. In 1990, Burtless assessed the fear that the U.S. job market would become dominated by low-skilled, low-wage work. His conclusion turned that fear on its head. "Ironically, [less-skilled workers'] labor market position could be improved if the U.S. economy produced *more* not fewer jobs requiring limited skill."[6]

What seemed like ivory tower logic was actually basic economics. The wage that a job pays is largely determined by supply and demand. In the early 1970s, a thirty-five-year-old man with a high school diploma averaged $35,000 per year (in year 2001 dollars). In the late 1980s, when Burtless was writing, a thirty-year-old man with a high school diploma averaged $30,000 per year (the same $30,000 figure holds today.)[7] In the interim, the number of traditional jobs for male high school graduates had grown slowly—more slowly than the number of men who wanted them. Wages of less educated workers declined as men (and women) competed for the jobs that were left. The same declining demand helps to explain why Mary Simmons and her fellow operators were not in a position to reject the computer monitoring of their work.

THE DETAILS OF ECONOMIC PROGRESS

Given these problems, we might ask why U.S. presidents routinely embrace new technology and expanded trade (of which outsourcing is a part)? The long-run answer is clear: technology and trade are both engines of economic growth that ultimately raise the national standard of living. We need only go back to 1929 when life expectancy was twenty years less than it is today to illustrate the point. But getting to the long run can be messy since economic growth in the short run usually creates losers as well as winners.[8]

During the industrial revolution, the short-run impact of growth was almost the opposite of what we see today. Technology favored not high-skilled workers but low-skilled workers as machines combined with unskilled labor to make products ranging from textiles to bicycles to guns. It was higher-skilled workers—weavers, clock makers, and other craftsmen—whom the technology displaced.

In some later periods, technology distributed its benefits more evenly. When John Kennedy was president, he could say "a rising tide lifts all the boats"[9] and be substantially correct. Kennedy governed in a lucky economic time when technology and trade did not strongly favor one skill group over another, and when economic growth raised incomes for most workers, even in the short run.

Today, politicians still invoke Kennedy's language, but that language no longer applies. As we have seen, the forces of economic growth now increase demand for highly skilled workers while they reduce demand for less skilled workers. In Ronald Reagan's eight years in office, the nation's Gross Domestic Product grew by 23 percent while the earnings of the average thirty-year-old male high school graduate fell by almost one-sixth and the college/high school earnings differential grew from 20 to 45 percent. During Bill Clinton's first term, the earnings of high school graduates fell still more. While these earnings recovered modestly in the boom of Clinton's second term, the college/high school differential continued to grow. The growth continued during the recent recession as the earnings of college graduates rose slightly and the earnings of high school graduates held steady. We predict that this technological bias against less skilled workers will continue for at least the next decade.

Sustained shifts in the demand for labor lack the drama of mass unemployment. But these shifts, if ignored, can lead to extraordinary pain for many workers and can ultimately threaten the fabric of our society. In the current situation, one bad outcome would be a hardening of the lines dividing economic classes. The process is easy to imagine. As income gaps expand, human nature dictates that higher income groups see that they have less in common with the rest of the population. In a political process that is responsive to money, the lack of perceived common interests translates into less redistribution and less protection for workers who are losing ground. As technology tilts the playing field against less-educated workers, these policy changes would tilt it further, reducing individual opportunity and upward mobility.

In a different, but equally bad outcome, job loss and insecurity would fuel a political movement to turn back the economic clock, for example, by imposing policies that restrict international trade. To the extent that these policies succeed, the result would be a frozen economic landscape that offers some short-run employment protection at the cost of long-run stagnation and decline.

HOW WINNERS TREAT LOSERS

As these possibilities illustrate, advances in computerization and computer-assisted trade have placed us in a potentially precarious position—one in which a significant fraction of workers is likely to experience economic hardship. There are no magic bullets here, but economic theory provides a useful way of thinking about these problems.

The argument is part of what is called Kaldor-Hicks improvements and begins by granting that economic growth can create losers as well as winners. Under these conditions, the argument goes, growth still represents a societal improvement—a gain in economic efficiency—if the winners could compensate the losers and still be better off themselves. The theory does not insist that compensation actually be paid, but that is the important social implication, with compensation coming through government taxes and expenditures or private charity. Compensation will not come through the market since the market is creating the winners and losers in the first place.

Why should the better-off pay compensation through taxes or charity? Why should families earning over $200,000 per year agree to higher taxes to subsidize healthcare for lower income families? Kaldor and Hicks were writing in terms of economic fairness but today their ideas can also be justified through enlightened self-interest. Our market economy exists in a framework of institutions that requires the political consent of the governed. People doing well today have a strong interest in preserving this consent. If enough people come to see the U.S. job market as stacked against them, the nation's institutions will be at great risk.

Examples of compensation include family health insurance coverage and retraining opportunities coupled with temporary income support.[10] Equally important are policies to improve life chances for the next generation, especially intensive efforts to improve education so that the children of today's workers will be in a stronger position to earn a decent living.

In economic terms, improved education is required to restore the labor market to balance. Recall Burtless's point—the falling wages of lower skilled jobs reflect the fact that demand was not keeping up with supply. If our predictions are right, this trend will continue as blue-collar and clerical jobs continue to disappear.

Better education is an imperfect tool for this problem. The job market is changing fast and improving education is a slow and difficult process (chapter 8). Even the best education cannot reach everyone. Nonetheless, over the long run, better education is the best tool we have to prepare the population for a rapidly changing job market.

Beyond economics, better education is also needed to prepare us for what will be a challenging political time. In less than a decade, computers have raised many workplace issues: wage inequality, the monitoring of work, lack of employee privacy, and a never-ending workday in which cell phones place employees constantly on call. These issues are not new. What is new is the increasing power of information technology to intrude on the lives of every citizen and the growing complexity of the social issues.

In the past, Americans have used the political process to address such issues through laws that guarantee the right to bargain collectively, that mandate overtime pay, and that regulate the use of surveillance technologies. Many of these new problems are candidates for legislation as well since they require collective solutions—a firm may be willing to drop intensive employee monitoring only if it is assured that other firms are dropping it as well.

Historically we have relied on our educational system both to prepare people to earn a living and to teach them the values, knowledge, and skills to participate in a democratic society. Because both goals are increasingly important, it is reasonable to ask whether we are asking schools to do too much—whether one agenda must now crowd out the other?

We believe the answer is no. The skills needed to excel at expert thinking and complex communication—the job skills that will grow in importance—are not specific subjects that compete for instructional time with social studies and science and other subjects in the standard school curricula. Rather they are strategies for tackling problems that cannot be solved by applying a set of rules. And they are also strategies for helping others to make sense of the many kinds of information to which we are all exposed. Expert thinking and complex communication are what students need to learn to do in studying science and history. As one example, in the field of genetics, students need to understand that the same advances in biology that make it possible to treat previously incurable genetic diseases also make possible "customized offspring," which in turn raise complex ethical and social issues.

The skills critical to expert thinking and complex communication are just as important to meeting these goals as they are to earning a living in a work world filled with computers.

CONCLUSION: THE FOUR QUESTIONS

There was a time, not so long ago, when the economy exhibited a comforting regularity. The unemployment rate moved through recessions and expansions but the same jobs that were lost on downturns were largely replaced on the upturns. Because the job market was fairly stable, the policies that interacted with the job market—the tax system, education, training—could be stable as well.

That world is largely gone now. Many of the jobs lost in the post-2000 recession—clerical and factory jobs lost to automation, call center jobs lost to India, manufacturing jobs lost to China—will not be coming back. This dynamic environment requires new policies and the first step in creating new policies is to recognize our new situation.

In chapter 1, we listed a set of four questions this book was designed to answer:

- What kinds of tasks do humans perform better than computers?
- What kinds of tasks do computers perform better than humans?
- In an increasingly computerized world, what well-paid work is left for people to do both now and in the future?
- How can people learn the skills to do this work?

Thirty years ago, we would have dismissed these questions as science fiction. Today, we seem more willing to listen. By keeping the four questions in front of us, we will be better able to appreciate the challenge we face as we work to progress as a nation.

NOTES

CHAPTER 1. New Divisions of Labor

1. Quoted from http://www.pa.msu.edu/people/mulhall/mist/Triple.html.

2. Adam Smith, *An Inquiry into the Nature and Causes of the Wealth of Nations* (New York: Modern Library, 1994; orig. 1776). Smith used the term to describe the increased efficiency that came when a particular job—making a straight pin, in his example—was divided into a series of narrow tasks—making the heads of pins, making the stems, sharpening the points—with each task assigned to a specialized worker.

3. On the increase in the number of the working poor, see Barbara Ehrenreich, *Nickel and Dimed: On (Not) Getting By in America* (New York: Owl Books, 2001).

4. One of a limited number of exceptions was the mechanical calculator, which could perform basic arithmetic.

5. Strictly speaking, the determining factor is not humans' absolute advantage but humans' comparative advantage. We discuss this issue in chapter 3.

6. Jeremy Rifkin, *The End of Work: The Decline of the Global Labor Force and the Dawn of the Post-Market Era* (New York: Putnam, 1995), xvii.

7. On re-engineering, see Michael Hammer, "Don't Automate, Obliterate," *Harvard Business Review* 68, no. 4 (July 1, 1990): 104–12. On the impact of e-commerce on sales jobs, see quotation attributed to Neil Rackham in Weld Royal, "Death of Salesmen," *Industry Week* 248, no. 10 (May 17, 1999): 59–66.

8. Peter F. Drucker, *The Practice of Management* (New York: Harper, 1954), 22.

9. Herbert A. Simon, "The Corporation: Will It Be Managed by Machines?" in *Management and the Corporations, 1985*, ed. M. L. Anshen and G. L. Bach (New York: McGraw-Hill, 1960), 38.

CHAPTER 2. Why People Still Matter

This chapter draws heavily on discussions with our colleague David Autor of MIT's Department of Economics. Some of the chapter's arguments first appeared in David H. Autor, Frank Levy, and Richard J. Murnane, "The Skill Content of Recent Technological Change: An Empirical Exploration," *Quarterly Journal of Economics* 118, no. 4 (November 2003): 1279–1333.

1. See Silvia Ascarelli, "Derivatives Traders Struggle to Grasp the Meaning of Life," *Wall Street Journal Europe*, November 19, 1999, 1.
2. Ibid.
3. On the gain in speed from the telegraph, see Daniel E. Sichel, *The Computer Revolution: An Economic Perspective* (Washington, D.C.: Brookings Institution, 1997). The telegraph allowed railroads to build new lines using one set of tracks with sidings rather than two full sets of tracks running in opposite directions—a cost savings that accelerated railroad expansion. On this cost savings and the first just-in-time inventory systems, see Alexander J. Field, "Modern Business Enterprise as a Capital-Saving Innovation," *Journal of Economic History* 37 (June 1987): 473–85.
4. The software treats the grandchild's picture as a fine grid. The stream of information is a code that specifies the color and intensity at each point on the grid—a hyper painting-by-numbers. Given enough time, a human could translate this code and create the picture.
5. This would be true whether the rules were applied one at a time by a human underwriter or by a computerized underwriter.
6. We thank Fannie Mae for allowing us to use Desktop Underwriter as an example. This does not constitute Fannie Mae's endorsement of any of the statements made in this book.
7. Technically, the statistical method was a probit analysis, a multiple-regression-like technique appropriate in situations in which the variable to be explained has only two values (represented as 1 or 0).
8. There is a final twist to the story. During the period of changeover, traders argued that dealers sitting at terminals would miss the buzz on the floor, which gave a feeling for the short run direction of the market. Increasingly, however, dealers were trading on the basis of computerized models that took no account of the buzz and so they saw no downside to foregoing it.
9. Michael Polanyi, *The Tacit Dimension* (New York: Doubleday, 1966), 4.
10. The exception was the software's voice recognition capabilities, which processed information by pattern recognition, a subject we later discuss.
11. See http://ist-socrates.berkeley.edu/~hdreyfus/html/paper_socrates.html.
12. This experiment is described in Hubert L. Dreyfus and Stuart E. Dreyfus, "From Socrates to Expert Systems: The Limits and Dangers of Calculative Rationality," available at http://ist-socrates.berkeley.edu/~hdreyfus/html/paper_socrates.html.
13. An example of this controversy based on infants' acquisition of language is found

in Gary F. Marcus, "Rule Learning by Seven-Month-Old Infants and Neural Networks," *Science* 283, no. 77 (1999), followed by the technical comment on Marcus's article by Gerry T. M. Altmann and Zoltán Dienes, and Marcus's reply to Altman and Dienes, both in *Science* 284 (1999): 875. The pieces can be accessed on the web by going to http://www.sciencemag.org/search.dtl and searching under G. Marcus.

14. On case-based reasoning, see Alan M. Lesgold, "The Nature and Methods of Learning by Doing" (mimeo, School of Education, University of Pittsburgh, May 2, 2002).

15. The goddaughter, Devorah "Debbie" Knaff, was, until recently, a cultural writer for the *Riverside Press Enterprise.*

16. "Learning" in this case involves estimating the probabilistic rules that predict potentially cancerous cell groupings based on geometric features of an image. ImageChecker is a product of R2 Technologies in Sunnyvale, California.

17. The author of the quote is Dr. Timothy W. Freer, Director of the Women's Diagnostic and Breast Health Center in Plano, Texas. The quote originally appeared in the journal *Radiology Today* and was reprinted on R2 Technology's website, http://www.r2tech.com/index2.html.

18. For a discussion of this approach to processing, see Rodney A. Brooks, *Cambrian Intelligence: The Early History of the New AI* (Cambridge: MIT Press, Bradford Books, 1999).

19. Jupiter Research press release, May 19, 2003: "Jupiter Research Forecasts Online Air Ticket Sales to Grow 14% despite War and Threat of SARS." Found at the following website: http://www.internet.com/corporate/releases/03.05.19-newjupresearch.html.

CHAPTER 3. How Computers Change Work and Pay

1. Kark Sabbagh, *21st-Century Jet: The Making and Marketing of the Boeing 777* (New York: Scribner, 1996), 58–59.

2. See http://www.boeing.com/commercial/777family/compute/index.html.

3. See Frances Cairncross, *The Death of Distance: How the Communications Revolution Will Change Our Lives* (Cambridge: Harvard Business School Press, 1997).

4. A larger fraction of the entire population was working in the year 2000 than in 1969, but the unemployment rate is defined as:

$$\frac{\text{(number of people looking for work)}}{\text{(number of people looking for work + number of people working)}},$$

and this statistic could be equal in the two years because the number of people working and the number of people looking for work had both risen.

5. Another factor contributing to the growth in the number of mutual funds was the replacement of defined benefit pension plans (fully managed by employers) by 401K plans.

6. These stories should be abstracted from temporary unemployment due to fluctuations in the business cycle.

7. That is, 50 percent of all families had higher incomes and 50 percent had lower incomes. The figure refers to all U.S. families regardless of age, the number of earners, etc.

8. Daniel E. Hecker, "Occupational Employment Projections to 2010," *Monthly Labor Review* 57, no. 84 (2001): p. 80, table 4.

9. The calculations that underlie figures 3.1 and 3.2 were done using the March supplements to the 1970 and 2000 Current Population Series. We included farmers and members of the armed forces in the total number of adult workers, but did not form separate categories for these very small groups.

10. Most blue-collar occupations are in manufacturing and construction but some—telephone repairmen, airline and bus mechanics—are found in service industries.

11. A more detailed analysis of sales employment shows a slight decline during the 1990s, but the thirty-year trend is strongly positive.

12. For a thoughtful discussion of the many definitions that the term "skill" can take, see Paul Attewell, "What Is Skill?" *Work and Occupations* 17, no. 4 (1990): 422–48.

13. It is also true that these face-to-face jobs must be performed where the customers are and so cannot be outsourced to other countries.

14. See Autor, Levy, and Murnane, "The Skill Content of Recent Technological Change," for evidence on the role of computers in bringing about these economic changes.

15. Over the past thirty years, the average U.S. wage grew very slowly, a reflection of slow-growing productivity. If the average wage had grown faster, high school graduates might have seen their wages hold steady or increase modestly while college graduates would have seen their wages increase rapidly.

16. The dollar figure on per-employee expenditures on training per year is taken from the following American Association for Training and Development website: http://www.astd.org/virtual_community/library/tfaq.html.

17. This work is detailed in Autor, Levy, and Murnane, "The Skill Content of Recent Technological Change."

18. A complete translation would also include changes in tasks that occur within occupations. See ibid. for a detailed description of the use we made of the data from the *Dictionary of Occupational Titles*.

19. See ibid. for a detailed description of the metric used on the vertical axis in figure 3.5.

20. For a detailed description of the methodology used in all the statistical work described in this chapter, including this test, see ibid.

21. To simplify exposition, we did not include in figure 3.6 the two bars displaying changes in nonroutine manual tasks. The two bars both have negative heights of −0.90, showing that over this period the percentage of the labor force working at nonroutine manual tasks fell, but that the decline was no more pronounced in computer-intensive industries than in other industries.

22. The name of the bank is fictitious to preserve confidentiality.

CHAPTER 4. Expert Thinking

1. The name of both the technician and the automobile brand are fictitious to preserve confidentiality.

2. These experiments are described in chapter 2 of J. Bransford, A. Brown, and R.

Cocking, eds., *How People Learn: Brain, Mind, Experience, and School* (Washington, D.C.: National Academy Press, 1999).

3. Or perhaps it could be reduced to rules—recall the case of the mortgage underwriter described in chapter 2.

4. John Seely Brown and Paul Duguid, *The Social Life of Information* (Cambridge: Harvard Business School Press, 2000), 101–2.

5. Marsden S. Blois, "Clinical Judgment and Computers," *New England Journal of Medicine* 303, no. 4 (July 24, 1980): 193.

6. The spark plug wires connect the top of each spark plug to the car's distributor, the rotating contact system that determines the order in which the cylinders fire.

7. An example of such a program is MYCIN, created at Stanford in the 1970s. Thanks go to Randy Davis, now at MIT and one of the creators of MYCIN, for recounting this history.

8. This example is taken from National Research Council, *Knowing What Students Know: The Science and Design of Educational Assessment*, ed. James Pellegrino, Naomi Chudowsky, and Robert Glaser (Washington, D.C.: National Academy Press, 2001).

9. George A. Miller, "The Magical Number Seven, Plus or Minus Two: Some Limits on Our Capacity for Processing Information," *Psychological Review* 63 (1956): 81–97.

10. The observation was made by the German physiologist Dietrich Trincker, as quoted in Tor Norretranders, *The User Illusion: Cutting Consciousness Down to Size* (New York: Viking Penguin, 1991), 126.

11. While "Andy Cooper" is the name of a real person, "Recruit.ASP" is a fictitious name.

12. For the same idea in a different context, see Donald A. Schon, *The Reflective Practitioner: How Professionals Think in Action* (New York: Basic Books, 1983).

13. See for example, Abraham Bernstein, "How Can Cooperative Work Tools Support Dynamic Group Processes? Bridging the Specificity Frontier," in *Proceedings of the ACM Conference on Computer Supported Cooperative Work (CSCW) 2000* (Philadelphia: Association for Computing Machinery, forthcoming).

14. Wanda J. Orlikowski, "Evolving with Notes: Organizational Change around Groupware Technology," in *Groupware and Teamwork: Invisible Aid or Technical Hindrance*, ed. Claudio U. Ciborra (New York: Wiley, 1996).

15. Equally thorny problems are the "lessons learned" databases where employees are encouraged to document their own mistakes (rather than a technician documenting a design or manufacturing mistake). However sound the ultimate insight, many employees are afraid of admitting a mistake in the first place. At Xerox and Orbit motors, service technicians were often describing problems that arose from faulty design or manufacturing—mistakes made by others. The incentive problem is harder when employees are asked to describe insights from their own mistakes.

16. Employees engaged in an eighty-hour round of initial training (forty hours in the classroom and forty hours on the job) to learn the skills needed to handle the full range of exceptions.

17. The acquisition of another bank led to a subsequent increase in the number of exceptions processed by the bank and the number of employees in exceptions processing.

18. For a detailed description of the Cabot Bank case, see David H. Autor, Frank Levy,

and Richard J. Murnane, "Upstairs, Downstairs: Computers and Skills on Two Floors of a Large Bank," *Industrial and Labor Relations Review* 55, no. 3 (2002).

CHAPTER 5. Complex Communication

1. As reported in Norretranders, *The User Illusion*, 91–92.

2. Why does a question mark or exclamation point represent seven bits of information? In Hugo's day, written language was based on sixty-five or seventy characters: letters (lowercase and capital), question marks, periods, the circumflex, the left parenthesis, and so on. The number of bits in a character refers to the number of (0,1) elements needed to construct a unique code for each character. A single bit can assume two values—0 and 1—and so could represent two characters: say, 0 = A and 1 = a. Two bits can form four distinct combinations (00, 01, 10, 11) and so could represent four characters: 00 = A, 01 = a, 10 = B, and so on. Six bits can form sixty-four distinct combinations, which is a little too small for our purposes, but seven bits can form 128 combinations, which is certainly adequate to identify each character that Hugo was using.

3. See Joseph LeDoux, *The Emotional Brain* (New York: Simon and Schuster, Touchstone, 1996).

4. David A. Friedman and Steven C. Currall, "Email Escalation: Dispute-Exacerbating Elements of Electronic Communication" (undated working paper, Vanderbilt University).

5. Malcolm Gladwell, "Clicks and Mortar—Don't Believe the Internet Hype: The Real E-Commerce Revolution Happened Offline," *New Yorker*, December 6, 1999.

6. Without the company's good reputation, the guarantee would have counted for little.

7. The exchange was generated on a web-based version of Eliza: http://www.manifestation.com/neurotoys/eliza.php3, accessed April 14, 2003. As Weizenbaum recounts, some people were quite seduced by Eliza and felt it could provide psychotherapy for the masses. See Joseph Weizenbaum, *Computer Power and Human Reason: From Judgment to Calculation* (San Francisco: Freeman, 1976).

8. One attempt to build trust without speech is contained in Glen L. Urban, Fareena Sultan, and William Qualls, "Placing Trust at the Center of Your Internet Strategy," *Sloan Management Review* 42, no. 1 (Fall 2000): 39–48.

9. As of this writing, the state of the art in conversational speech recognition is AT&T's "How May I Help You?" software for customer service calls. See www.research.att.com./~algor/hmihy.

10. There are many variations of this sentiment—e.g., "They don't care what you know until they know that you care."

11. Nicholas Murray, *The Excellent Investment Advisor* (self-published, 1996), 134.

12. Names of the brokers and the city have been changed to preserve confidentiality. Many brokers within major brokerage houses are organized into small (three to eight person) semi-independent operations that share commissions with the brokerage house in exchange for office space, computer facilities, etc.

13. See, for example, Paul Ekman, *Telling Lies: Clues to Deceit in the Marketplace, Politics and Marriage* (New York: Norton, 2001). In fact, we are not as adept at processing this information as we think we are. For example, a person's avoidance of direct eye contact while speaking is not a good indication that he or she is lying.

14. For experimental evidence on this point, see Kathleen Valley, Leigh Thompson, Robert Gibbons, and Max H. Bazerman, "How Communication Improves Efficiency in Bargaining Games," *Games and Economic Behavior* 38 (2002): 127–55.

15. See Guy Moszkowski et al., *Online Broker Quarterly*, February 13, 2003, and *The Online Broker Rankings*, November 5, 2001, published by Salomon Smith Barney Equity Research, New York City. The declining share of e-trades reflected the desire for human advisors and the fact that a number of day-traders left the market.

16. The reason why Dan's goal was the growth of Lisa's assets is that his annual payment was a fixed percentage of the value of the assets.

17. Patsy and John Ryder and Frank Sylvan are pseudonyms, but Elliot Mahler is the name of the lawyer who mediated this dispute.

18. Frederick W. Taylor, *The Principles of Scientific Management* (New York: Norton. 1967; orig. 1911), 45.

19. Brown and Duguid, *The Social Life of Information*, 94.

CHAPTER 6. Enabling Skills

1. The name Mary Simmons is a pseudonym.

2. The description of customer service representatives' work in the telecommunications industry draws from Rosemary Batt, Larry W. Hunter, and Steffanie Wilk, "How and When Does Management Matter? Job Quality and Career Opportunities for Call Center Workers," in *Low Wage America* (New York: Russell Sage Foundation, 2003).

3. Quotation is from Orlikowski, "Evolving with Notes: Organizational Change around Groupware Technology."

4. There is a great deal of thoughtful writing on the changing definition of literacy. For example, see the many articles by University of Pittsburgh Professor Lauren B. Resnick, including "Literacy in School and Out," *Daedalus* 119, no. 2 (Spring 1990): 169–85.

5. See Richard J. Murnane, John B. Willett, and Frank Levy, "The Growing Importance of Cognitive Skills in Wage Determination," *Review of Economics and Statistics* 77, no. 2 (1995): 251–66.

6. See, for example, the Secretary's Commission on Achieving Necessary Skills, *What Work Requires of Schools: A SCANS Report for America 2000* (Washington, D.C.: U.S. Department of Labor, June 1991).

7. See Eric Neuberger, *Home Computers and Internet Use in the United States: August 2000*, Current Population Reports (U.S. Census Bureau, 2001).

8. Several subsequent studies using different data and different methodologies support the DiNardo and Pischke interpretation. For example, see John P. Haisken-Denew and Christoph M. Schmidt, "Money for Nothing and Your Chips for Free? The Anatomy of the PC Wage Differential" (IZA Discussion Paper no. 86, Bonn, Germany, December 1999). Harry A. Krashinsky, "Do Marital Status and Computer Usage Really Change the Wage Structure? Evidence from a Sample of Twins" (Princeton University, Industrial Relations Section, Working Paper no. 439).

9. National Research Council, *Being Fluent with Information Technology* (Washington, D.C.: National Academy Press, 1999).

CHAPTER 7. Computers and the Teaching of Skills

1. This discussion is an example of case-based reasoning (chapter 2). A manager might never have a direct report exactly like Ned, but the ideas she would learn from discussing with others Alonzo's problem with Ned would help build patterns of knowledge—schemas—that she could adapt to similar problems.

2. Todd Willis is a pseudonym for one of the participants in Basic Blue.

3. See Mary Ann Zehr, "Computer Giants Look to Students," *Education Week* 17, no. 31 (April 15, 1998).

4. For the details of this story, see Richard Murnane, Nancy Sharkey, and Frank Levy, "A Role for the Internet in American Education? Lessons from Cisco Networking Academies," in *The Knowledge Economy and Postsecondary Education*, ed. Patricia Albjerg Graham and Nevzer G. Stacey (Washington, D.C.: National Academy Press, 2002), 127–57.

5. As discussed later, the community server also keeps track of students' grades on chapter tests and the semester examination, eliminating the bookkeeping activities that consume a great deal of time for most teachers.

6. For rich discussions of the asymmetric information and self-selection ideas, see Daron Acemoglu and Jorn-Steffan Pischke, "Beyond Becker: Training in Imperfect Labour Markets," *Economic Journal* 109, no. 453 (February 1999): F112–42; and David Autor, "Why Do Temporary Help Firms Provide Free General Skills Training?" *Quarterly Journal of Economics* 116, no. 4 (November 2001): 1409–48.

CHAPTER 8. Standards-Based Education Reform in the Computer Age

1. The wage data come from the following Economic Policy Institute website: http://www.epinet.org/content.cfm/datazone_dznational.

2. Expessed in constant 2000–01 dollars, the relevant numbers are $4,427 for the 1969–70 school year and $7,653 for the 1989–90 school year. These figures are taken from the *Digest of Education Statistics 2001*, p. 191, table 167.

3. The $12 billion figure represents the cumulative increase in state aid during the 1994–2003 period over the 1993 level. The figure is not inflation-adjusted. We are indebted to Robert Costrell for providing this information.

4. The Massachusetts Common Core of Learning, available at: http://www.doe.mass.edu/edreform/commoncore/thinking.html.

5. The only questions not made public were those being tried out for possible inclusion in the next year's exams. Students' scores on these questions did not count toward their grade on the exams.

6. This information is taken from the following U.S. Department of Education website: http://nces.ed.gov/nationsreportcard/writing/results2002/stateachieve-g8-compare.asp.

7. William L. Taylor, "Standards, Tests, and Civil Rights," *Education Week* 20, no. 11 (November 15, 2000): 56, 40–41.

8. H. F. Ladd and R. P. Walch, "Implementing Value-Added Measures of School Effectiveness: Getting the Incentives Right," *Economics of Education Review* 21 (2001).

9. Kathryn M. Doherty and Ronald A. Skinner, "State of the States," *Education Week* 22, no. 17 (January 9, 2003): 75–105.

10. Lynn Olson, "States Debate Exam Policies for Diplomas," *Education Week* 22, no. 36 (May 14, 2003): 1, 22.

11. This information is taken from the following U.S. Department of Education website: http://www.ed.gov/offices/OESE/esea/exec-summ.html.

CHAPTER 9. The Next Ten Years

1. The evidence suggests that a significant fraction of all older, male high school drop-outs have gone on the disability rolls. See David H. Autor and Mark G. Duggan, "The Rise in Disability Rolls and the Decline in Unemployment" *Quarterly Journal of Economics* 118, no. 1 (February 2003): 157–205.

2. This discussion draws heavily on Victor W. Zue and James R. Glass, "Conversational Interfaces: Advances and Challenges," in *Spoken Language Processing,* a special issue of *Proceedings of the IEEE* (August 2000): 1166–80.

3. See, for example, Amy Waldman, "More 'Can I Help You?' Jobs Migrate from U.S. to India," *New York Times*, May 11, 2003, 4.

4. Ibid.

5. In the longer run, as demand increases, foreign programming wages may well rise.

6. Gary Burtless "Introduction" and "Summary," in *A Future of Lousy Jobs?* ed. Gary Burtless (Washington, D.C.: Brookings Institution, 1990), 30.

7. Annual income estimates based on hourly wage figures contained in Lawrence Mishel, Jared Bernstein, and Heather Boushey, *The State of Working America 2002–3* (Ithaca: Cornell University Press, ILR Press, 2003), table 2.21.

8. Long-term growth refers to the long-term trend in incomes over several decades, a trend that explains why people today have higher incomes than people who lived fifty years ago. The year-to-year path of incomes cycles around this long-term trend, moving below the trend in recession and above the trend in boom times.

9. A researcher at the John F. Kennedy Library has told us that Kennedy used this phrase at a number of times and in slightly different versions. The library's earliest record of the phrase was on October 15, 1960, during Kennedy's presidential campaign.

10. See, for example, the discussion of livelihood insurance in Robert J. Shiller, *The New Financial Order: Risk in the 21st Century* (Princeton: Princeton University Press, 2003).

9. [illegible] "[illegible]," [illegible] 12 (January 9, 2000), p. 103.

10. [illegible], "Street [illegible] for [illegible]," [illegible], 18 May 1998, p. 22.

11. The information is taken from the following US Department [illegible] website: [illegible]

CHAPTER 9. The New Territory

1. The evidence [illegible] significant [illegible] [illegible] [illegible] the [illegible] [illegible] [illegible] and the Decline [illegible] [illegible] [illegible] (Autumn 2000): [illegible]

2. This [illegible] [illegible] [illegible] [illegible] [illegible]

3. See, for example, [illegible] "US [illegible]," *New York Times*, May 15, 2000, A[illegible].

4. Ibid.

5. In the [illegible] [illegible] [illegible] [illegible]

6. Gary Burtless, [illegible] (Washington, D.C.: Brookings Institution, 1999), 35.

7. [illegible] (Ithaca: Cornell University Press, 2000), [illegible].

8. [illegible] [illegible] [illegible] [illegible] below the [illegible] [illegible] [illegible].

9. [illegible] [illegible] [illegible] [illegible] phrase [illegible] [illegible] [illegible].

10. See, for example, [illegible] *The New Financial Order* [illegible] (Princeton: Princeton University Press, 2003).

INDEX